BASEBALL

BASEBALL

DPH SPORTS SERIES

BASEBALL

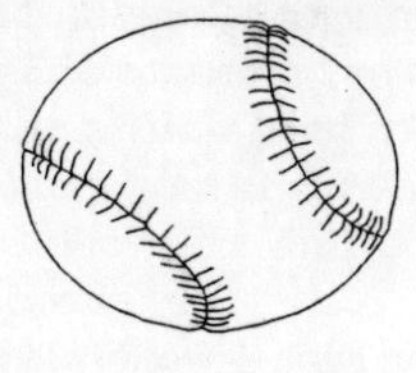

H. C. Dubey

DISCOVERY PUBLISHING HOUSE
New Delhi-110002

ISBN: 978-81-7141-473-4

Baseball

Published by:
DISCOVERY PUBLISHING HOUSE PVT. LTD.
4383/4B, Ansari Road, Darya Ganj
New Delhi-110 002 (India)
Phone: +91-11-23279245, 43596064-65
Fax: +91-11-23253475
E-mail: discoverypublishinghouse@gmail.com
sales@discoverypublishinggroup.com
web: www.discoverypublishinggroup.com

Printed at:
Infinity Imaging Systems
Delhi

PREFACE

The need of having a sports series felt because today's situation of the world is not conducive to peace, all round there is destruction, despair, conflict and war; war if not between two nations then within the country itself. In a world where there are some 820 million people unemployed or under-employed, and where 86 million people are born every year, it is not surprising that one out of every four individuals lives in absolute poverty. The *Discovery Publishing House* by Publishing this series seeks to get positive response as—to means by which sports can promote and propagate peace and international cooperation. Sportsmen form a large identifiable cadre. We visualises a situation where a conscious efforts is made all over the world to train the sportspersons to spread the message of peace and international cooperation. Instead of peace keeping efforts through arms and army, the sportspersons may be used as soldiers of peace in a subtle manner. The effort is to make the realize the contribution of sports as a factor for sustainable development, peace keeping and international cooperation.

In developing countries, sports development cooperation is still in the need of justification and steadfast arguments. Many people ask the question "why invest in sports in developing countries for which water supply, health service and agriculture projects are much better suited? An apt reply to this question may be "for many of the people of a developing country,

Sports is the only 'Sweaty' Leisure-time activity. Sports represents a moment of joy in the midst of hard poverty-stricken and dirty everyday life. Doing sports even makes one's work go more smoothly the next day.

This series will be useful to the sports promoters, organisers, coaches and other persons related or interested in sports.

Editor

CONTENTS

1 INTRODUCTION

Derived from the English children's game of rounders, baseball is today the national game of the United States and the principal summer game of Canada, Japan, and several Latin-American countries.

The four basic skills of greatest importance in baseball are throwing (which includes pitching), catching, batting, and base running.

Throwing

The objective in throwing is to move the ball from one point to some other specified point in the shortest possible time (in fielding) or with the optimum linear and angular velocities (in pitching).

Fielding. The time taken in moving the ball from one point to another is the sum of the time taken to execute the throwing movement (that is, from initiation of the movement until the ball is released) and the time of flight. The first of these depends on the average speed of the ball during the throwing movement (which is, in turn, governed by the magnitude and direction of the forces exerted upon the ball and the times for which they act) and by the distance through which the ball moves. The second is governed by the velocity and height of release and, to some extent, by air resistance.

Pitching. Since the ball is initially at rest in the pitcher's glove, the linear velocity that it possesses as it leaves his hand on its way to the strike zone is directly related to the forces applied to it during the act of pitching. As the work-energy relationship suggests, the velocity at release is also related to the distance over which the various forces are applied. The pertinence of this parameter is reflected, for example, in the long stride that pitchers use to ensure that the distance over which forces are applied is as large as it can be, consistent with other requirements and limitations.

The angular velocity with which the ball leaves the pitcher's hand depends on the torque applied to it during the release. Ignoring slight variations in the moment arm due to the seams, the magnitude of this torque is directly related to the magnitudes and directions of the forces exerted on the ball via the pitcher's fingers. In practice, these forces are a function of the grip employed and the actions of the pitcher's wrist and fingers during the release. The magnitude and direction of the angular velocity of the ball largely determines the extent to which the Magnus effect operates and hence the amount to which the ball can be made to deviate from its normal parabolic flight path. The successful pitching of curves, sliders, and so on is thus very dependent on the optimum angular velocity being obtained at the moment of release.

Catching

The objective here is to take hold of a ball flying through the air and to reduce its velocity to zero or near-zero. To achieve this objective a player must exert forces on the ball in a direction opposite to that in which it is travelling. In the process of exerting these

1

forces, the player's hands, the means by which the forces are transmitted, are subjected to a certain amount of pressure. The magnitude of this pressure on the hands largely determines the player's ability to "hold" the ball. If he attempts to catch the ball in such a manner that the pressure becomes intolerably large, the player suffers acute discomfort and perhaps even an injury to his hands. In addition, he is very likely to drop the ball, thereby completely negating his efforts. The pressure exerted on any part of the player's hands is dependent on the magnitude of the force being exerted on the hands and by the area over which this force is distributed. Thus, to avoid the undesirable consequences of having too great a pressure on the hands, players strive to decrease the force exerted and to increase the area over which this force is spread.

Batting

The objectives in batting are to hit the ball at will and to impart to it that velocity necessary to displace it to some specific point within (or outside!) the ball park. The displacement experienced by a batted ball may be thought of as the sum of two displacements--one resulting from its flight through the air and the other from the bouncing and rolling that it does once it strikes the ground. The first of these is governed by the height and velocity at which the ball leaves the bat and by the air resistance that it encounters in flight.

For all practical purposes the height of "release" (which is governed by the height of the ball as it enters or approaches the strike zone and by the height of pitch at which the batter prefers to swing) is of relatively minor importance. The velocity of "release," on the other hand, is all-important. This velocity is governed by the respective masses of the bat and ball, their respective velocities before impact, and their mutual coefficient of restitution. In practice, however, the batter has a measure of control over only three of these factors: the velocities of bat and ball before impact and the mass of the bat. Apart from the drag force, the principal effect that air resistance has on the flight of the ball is that due to the Magnus effect. Since this effect is due solely to the fact that the ball is spinning, the generally unwelcome deviations that result from it must be attributed to the factors that produce such spin.

The spin (or angular velocity) with which a ball leaves the bat can be regarded as the summed effect of the spin imparted to the ball by the pitcher (and over which the batter has no real control) and the spin imparted by the bat during its period of contact with the ball. This latter spin is the result of a frictional force that is created whenever the impact between bat and ball is an oblique on.

The bouncing-and-rolling displacement experienced by the ball depends on the velocity at which it strikes the ground (which, in turn, depends on the same factors that govern the flight displacement) and on the forces to which it is subsequently subjected.

Base running

A base runner's purpose is to traverse the distance from one base to the next without being tagged or thrown out. Apart from making the correct decision concerning whether or not he should run, the most important facet of his performance is the time he takes to cover the required distance. 'This time depends on the distance involved and on the average speed of the runner. A base runner's average speed is a function of his speed at all points on his run--his speed in starting, in running, and in sliding or stopping. His speed in starting, running, and stopping (like that of a runner on a track, football field, or basketball court) is equal to the product of his stride length and his rate of striding, or stride frequency. These in turn are determined very largely by the reaction to the forces that the runner exerts against the ground. A runner's speed in sliding is similarly governed by the reaction to the forces that he exerts against the ground.

2

PITCHING

In pitching, the name of the game is getting the ball over the plate with good stuff on it. These are still the essentials for pitching success. The better the stuff, the less important the control, providing the base on balls is not a factor. In looking over a young pitching prospect, major league scouts want to see that fast one move a little with good velocity. They want a boy who can throw hard because this is one thing they cannot teach a pitcher to do. With the excellent coaching of today, most pitchers with a good fast ball can be taught the other pitches. It is difficult to improve the fast ball very much unless the pitcher is doing something mechanically wrong in the delivery.

When we think of the pitching game, first we think of proper mechanics and control. Lack of control is generally the result of poor mechanics. Unless his mechanism is good, with everything working together, the pitcher will find it difficult to be "in a groove." With the tendency for pitchers to throw additional pitches, such as the slider, screwball, and a variety of changes, we think good mechanics are even more important.

There are three physical elements to a pitch. Velocity, movement, and location--and the least important of these is velocity. Pitching is location. A pitcher may have overwhelming stuff, but if he can't put the ball where he wants to, he will not be successful. A pitcher should also learn the value of changing speeds and varying the tempo to keep hitters off balance.

How can a young pitcher master control? There is only one solution: practice and more practice. Not Just throwing the ball, but throwing the ball to a target. Control comes to different people at different times. Sandy Koufax, for example, had to work very hard to get his control, but after years of frustration Sandy finally found the key. He discovered the method that put rhythm into his delivery, but it came only by working constantly, with Coach Joe Becker at his side.

Deception is another big factor in the makeup of a successful pitcher. Along with control and a strong, live arm, many authorities believe the key to pitching is deceiving the hitter. Confusing the hitter by throwing the ball at different speeds with the same motion, hiding it until the last possible moment, and using good judgment in the selection of pitches are other factors that can increase the pitcher's effectiveness.

Along with the physical aspects of pitching, mental attitude is essential to the success of a moundsman. Like his teammates, he must have confidence in himself, a positive feeling that he can do it. He must have a mental attitude that says, I know I can d: it." He must not let a bad pitch or a lost game discourage him. Command and poise are qualities possessed by the great pitchers in baseball. There pitchers have complete command of their actions in regard to their pitching mechanics. A pitcher has to have complete confidence that he will get them out, that he is better than the hitter. He must be in complete control.

We like to see a young pitcher concentrate on what he is trying to do. Whenever he throws the ball, he should have an idea where he wants to throw it. He has to block out everything except the job he is doing--getting the batter out. He must be alert all the time.

Rhythm and timing

Proper rhythm and timing are the basis of successful pitching. The purpose of rhythm and timing is to generate speed and momentum in the pitching arm. When a pitcher is throwing "heat," his timing is just right. On his off days, when his fast ball is just mediocre, he gives the impression of pushing or pulling the ball up to the plate.

Proper rhythm and timing can be achieved by developing good balance and body control, which enable the pitcher to transfer his weight at the proper time and create a consistent point of release. Arm speed and body momentum can be realized by getting the arm on top of the pitch--before the striding foot hits the ground.

The pitching greats of baseball, those who have stood up over a long period of time, display excellent rhythm and timing. Tom Seaver, Jim Palmer, Steve Carlton, and Jerry Reuss are modern-day hurlers who typify well coordinated pitching deliveries.

To have good rhythm and timing, a pitcher's gears have to be meshed. It is a case of meshing the arm and upper body with the striding leg and lower body. The upper and lower halves of the body should come through simultaneously like the parts of a machine working together. The result will be action with power. The greatest problem of most pitchers is rushing the delivery. If the body weight moves out in front too soon, a "rushing arm action" will develop, bringing about control problems and inconsistent power. Generally, when the leg stride is too quick, the pitcher has rushed his pitch, or his upper body is too slow. If the striding foot hits the ground and the throwing arm is way back, a pitcher has a pulling motion instead of action with power. The solution is to keep the weight back during the pivot until the pitching arm gets up on top. This will set the stage for the arm and body, to come through at the same time. In simple terms, weight retention actually means, "Don't run off and leave your arm." When the striding foot lands, the throwing arm is up on top in the proper position for delivering the ball on a downward plane.

Essentials of pitching

The three things we look for in young pitchers are ability to throw hard, a good live ball, and control. One has to have a good arm. Most big-league scouts use a grading system, and they look for the fellow who has an adequate major league fast ball. Control, the other top requirement, is perhaps the hardest fundamental to teach. Control means more than just throwing the ball into the strike zone. It means moving the ball around, in and out, up and down, keeping the batter constantly off balance. As he progresses in experience and skill, a pitcher will learn how to go to work on the hitter, trying to make him hit his best pitch.

Another requirement for successful pitching is that the pitcher have some off-speed pitches and be able to get them over. With hitting being so dependent on timing, off-speed pitches, such as a straight change or taking a little off the curve, can be highly effective. This is especially true today, when so many players are at the end of the bat. The harder they swing, the easier they sometimes are to fool with an off-speed pitch. The off-speed pitch does not strike the man out too often, but it will take some of his power and timing away.

What type of physical size do Dodger scouts look for in a pitcher? We prefer a well-built boy, with a long arm and supple muscles. Drysdale, perhaps, was the ideal size, although a pitcher does not have to be six feet three inches or six feet four inches. Drysdale had long, slender arms, the kind that do not become muscle-bound and provide the real good stuff on the ball. Tom Seaver, at six feet one inch and 205 pounds, has demonstrated not only explosive power but the strength and stamina to go all the way.

A pitcher should use a style of his own and throw naturally, providing, of course, he is not doing something fundamentally wrong. The arm angle, particularly, should be one which feels most comfortable and natural. The three-quarter overhand delivery is used most because it is the most natural delivery for the majority of pitchers.

The basic pitches

Through the years, Dodger pitchers have concentrated pretty much on the basic three pitches. We have had good luck, not having many fellows hurt themselves or develop sore arms.

High school pitchers, particularly, should stay with the fast ball, curve ball, and some change-of-pace, whether they take a little bit off the curve ball or throw a straight change. Quite often, a young pitcher thinks he needs another pitch, but, actually, he may not have good command of the pitches he has. He should not consider another pitch until the basic three can be delivered with control, consistency, and effectiveness.

After he progresses and cart control these pitches, the young pitcher might go to a different kind of curve ball or a slider. Lately, more pitchers are turning the ball over with a good sinker--a sinking fast ball thrown from a three-quarter or sidearm delivery. The pitcher uses a sweeping arm action across the body and cuts the ball at the last moment. If a fellow has a major league fast ball and curve ball, and a good change-up, and can control these pitches, getting them over pretty much when and where he wants to, we think he has enough to be a successful pitcher. Coming up with a couple of extra pitches is not the answer.

Pitchers today in the big leagues have a half-dozen different pitches in their repertoire. They throw a couple of different speeds on their curve ball, and they throw sliders. They turn the ball over on the sinker, screwball, or the change-of-pace. Pitchers who are not overpowering must rely on changing speeds and control.

The less power a pitcher possesses, the more important keeping the hitter off-stride is. However, it is possible to have too many pitches, as the refinement and control of each becomes more difficult with every new pitch added.

Seaver, of course, is the complete pitcher. He has low fast balls, one that rises, another that sinks. He has the ability to make his fast ball sink, sail, or tail, according to the way he holds the ball. Tom also has a good slider, a fine curve, and can change up on all of his pitches. The Little League pitcher, particularly, should rely almost completely on the fast ball. It is the only pitch with which he can strengthen his arm with minimum risk of injury.

The slider has attained considerable prominence among present-day major league pitchers. It is a fast ball with a break and is most effective when it breaks outside and hitters go reaching for it, or when it breaks in on a left-handed hitter. However, some coaches do not advise their young pitchers to throw it, claiming it is hard on the arms of some pitchers. Those who come up with sore arms usually throw the slider with a stiff wrist. The rigid wrist transfers strain to the elbow. This is why we advocate a loose wrist for the slider. Unfortunately, some pitchers substitute the slider for their curve ball, and they cease to use the curve and do not develop it.

"I like to see pitchers change their speeds more," said Red Adams, our pitching coach. "Off-speed pitches not only get the hitter off stride, but they provide some rest for the pitcher. They also complement the other stuff. Such pitches as the knuckleball and screwball should be used only by more experienced pitchers."

Young pitchers today are throwing too many breaking balls. Coaches on all levels have their pitchers throwing four pitches right away, and there is no question it eventually takes away velocity. Too many breaking balls can place a tremendous strain on the arm. The only way to stretch out the arm and get maximum velocity is to throw fast balls.

The pitcher should hold the ball so that it feels most comfortable and so that he gets the most life into his pitches. Ideally, the ball should be grasped in the same manner for each pitch, but this is not always possible.

We suggest that our pitchers try various grips and we let them decide which one feels the best. However, the way the seam is held is not as important as the way the ball is released.

Generally, a pitcher will grip the ball either across the seams or with the seams. If he is with the seams, there are two possibilities:

1. His fingers are at the narrow area where they come together.
2. He can slip on around a little further, where he can get the tip of his finger on the seams and still be with the seams.

For the pitcher with the three-quarter delivery, who does not have exceptional power, I would suggest that he grip the ball with the seams to get a little more movement out of the ball. The ball may sink for him when down, or tail in toward the hitter when up. Many pitchers grip the ball across the seams at the widest part. The second and third fingertips are placed on the seams, while the thumb is on the seam beneath the ball. Only a slight variation of finger movement is needed to throw the curve or slider. The thumb plays a very important role in all pitches, it can make the ball go one way or the other.

The cross-the-seams grip provides the most carry and the best control. With this grip, the power pitchers of baseball can actually make the ball take off vertically or rise. But those who are not power pitchers have greater flexibility using the with-the-seams grip. They will be able to learn a sinker or slider more effectively from this grip. Successful pitching demands an understanding of correct spin on the ball. "Spin the ball easily and get the ball to spin in the direction you want it to spin," explained Johnny Sain, former outstanding pitcher and a highly successful pitching coach. "Then, apply more spin, more spin, more spin, more spin, and more spin."

Many pitchers have improved noticeably by learning how to get better spin on the ball. Additional spin not only can improve breaking pitches but can make the fast ball livelier.

The spin on Warren Spahn's fast ball was amazing--a backward rotation which helped give the pitch its hop. "In order to develop more spin on a baseball," said Sain, "a pitcher has to learn the basic idea. And from here, he spins the ball easy, applying more spin and seed until he gets the ball doing what he likes."

The pitcher should try moving his thumb a little toward his hand or farther under the ball. Some tucking of the thumb will make him "cut" the ball a little causing a sinking movement.

In most cases, a pitcher who has trouble applying good spin grips the ball too tightly. When a pitcher grips the ball too tightly with his thump, it seems to lock his wrist. He does not have that loose, fast wrist and finger action. Actually, it is a combination of wrist and finger action that applies the spin to the ball.

Fast ball

There is no substitute for a good fast ball. Indeed, the king of all pitches is still the fast ball. A young pitcher would be wise to rely on his fast ball because of the strengthening effect on the arm. A good fast, ball comes off the end of a smooth delivery, a coordinated action of the entire body, in which the strong wrist and forearm play a vital role. To make the ball hop, a pitcher must provide backspin to the ball. He must exert strong pressure on his fingertips with his wrist, snapping down quickly as the ball leaves his hand.

The ball should be gripped as far out on the fingertips as possible. The wrist must remain relaxed in order to obtain the quick "forward" wrist snap so necessary. "When you overthrow on your fast ball, you can tense up your wrist," said Jim Palmer, one of modern baseball's most successful pitchers. The ball will lose its natural break and good snap because of the tight wrist.

There is no set way to throw the fast ball. The grip that gives the best results, of course, should be used. Generally, a two-seam grip will make the ball go down and away; four-seam grip--up and in. Many big-league pitchers throw two types of fast balls:

1. *Rising fast ball* (across the seams) The forefinger and middle finger grip the ball across one of the wide seams, at a point where the seams of the ball are farthest apart. The thumb is underneath. The ring finger and little finger are bent and curled under

the side of the ball. From this grip, the pitcher can get maximum action from the four long seams.

For a three-quarter overarm delivery, the ball is released out in front with a strong follow-through. When thrown by a right-handed pitcher, this fast ball has a tendency to ride in slightly on a right-handed hitter and away from a left-handed hitter. When thrown completely overarm by pitchers with good velocity, the fast ball tends to rise, thus earning its title as the "riser."

2. Sinking fast ball (*with the seams)* The "sinking" fast ball is released with an over-the-top, then outside-in, flip of the wrist. For a right-handed pitcher, this ball drives down and in on a right-handed hitter, and down and away from a left-handed swinger. In releasing the ball, the pitcher has to turn the ball over at the last moment, placing more pressure on the index finger.

This fast ball is gripped with the middle finger and forefinger curled snugly, not tightly, along the two parallel short seams.

Known as a sinker, it is a little more difficult to throw than the rising fast ball because of the over-the-top wrist flip. When a ground ball is needed, this pitch can be very effective.

The two things big-league pitching coaches look for is whether a pitcher's ball has good velocity and whether it moves. Some pitchers have good velocity but their fast ball does not move; it just comes in straight, on a line. Pitchers of small stature must have more body speed or momentum and extremely good rhythm in order to be fast enough.

Curve ball

"The key to a good curve ball is the snap," said Roger Craig, who had a great curve when he pitched for the Dodgers. "The curve ball has to be held very **loose** in your hand, not tight. The elbow has to be up, and a good hard snap has to be made at the release point The curve ball should be thrown with a little less speed than the fast ball, but with the same motion."

Some pitchers have a tendency to overthrow the curve. They either release the ball too far out in front and bounce it, or they try to throw the ball too hard. As a result, their front shoulder stays up and the ball is up in the hitter's eyes--it just spins.

"In developing a better wrist snap, it is very important to get the hand more on top of the ball, a more downward break and a tighter grip with the second finger," said Don McMahon. "By getting the hand in closer to the head, a pitcher can get more of a pull down and greater shoulder action."

Carl Erskine, a former Dodger who possessed an outstanding curve ball, always thought of tickling his ear when he threw the curve ball. This helped him keep his wrist tucked, in and provided good over-the-top spin on the ball. The more the arm is tucked in, the bigger the break. However, the fact that Erskine threw directly overhand should be kept in mind. Each individual should throw the curve ball from the same angle as his fast ball.

"The biggest factor with the curve is getting the ball down," says Warren Spahn, the former all time great southpaw. "The higher you let the ball go, the more chance you have of hanging it."

The curve is a pitch that should be thrown low. A high curve has a tendency to "hang," and a pitcher who keeps his curve high is simply asking for trouble. An ineffective curve often is caused by not pulling down on the ball enough or letting go of the ball too soon.

The grip is very important to a good curve ball. Most of the good breaking ball pitchers in the major leagues hold the ball with the four seams. "When they release the ball, the ball comes out and you have the four seams biting against the wind," said Craig. "This gives the ball a better bite and the good, tight spin on the ball which is hard for the hitter to pick up. If you hold the ball with the seams, only the two seams, the hitter sees more of the red seams of the ball, and it's easier to pick up. Whereas with the four seams, it is like a blur and is very difficult to pick up."

Throughout the delivery, the elbow has to stay at least parallel to the shoulder. When the elbow drops down below the shoulder, the pitcher cannot get the good power and snap.

The pitcher should wait until his arm is close, to the rear of his head before going into his curve ball. The wrist must be cocked back of the head. The elbow starts forward first, and the wrist turns over and snaps downward to put a rapid spin on the ball. "Turn, turn, and PULL DOWN!" describes the wrist and hand action in providing the greatest amount of spin. It is the spin given to the ball that makes it curve.

The wrist should be completely turned over after a very quick reverse snap. The ball is released over the first and second joints of the first finger--like a ball rolling off a table. The first two fingers are close, with the thumb extended and not curled. "Let go of it in front of you," describes the type of release necessary for the curve.

The longer the pitcher can wait, the better curve he will throw. He must stay on top of the ball and put great pressure or pull on his middle finger.

The middle finger is the pressure finger, the one that controls the seam and imparts much of the spin. The moment he starts coming down is when the pitcher must really pull down hard with a sweep of the arm across the body toward the opposite knee. The hand usually comes back toward the body, whereas the hand release on the fast ball is more toward the hitter. In releasing the ball, he should let it roll over on his index finger. This is how spin is imparted for a good breaking action of the curve ball.

Perfecting the curve ball requires a great amount of practice, learning how to coordinate the speed of spin, the angle of spin, and using a natural pitching motion.

Practice to get the correct spin. The pitcher should have a catcher stand fifteen to twenty feet away from him and just spin the ball into his glove.

Every pitcher at every level of baseball should have an off-speed pitch of some kind that he can get over the plate. A good change-up can be an extremely valuable asset to a pitcher. This is particularly true as he climbs higher in baseball. It takes courage to throw a change-up, but it is a pitch that must be learned and controlled by every pitcher. Without a good change-up, a pitcher is definitely limiting his baseball career. By perfecting the technique of his off-speed pitches, he will develop the confidence that he can use them effectively at any time. The change-up is particularly effective in disrupting the hitter's timing. When he is set for a fast ball, a change-up will likely cause the batter to place his weight on his front foot too soon. He will hit the ball with only an arm swing.

Typically, pitchers on the Baltimore Orioles throw as many as two dozen change-ups during a game. According to pitching coach Ray Miller, "An Orioles pitcher will start throwing them in the first inning to show the hitter he has it. He will also wind up throwing less pitches and staying fresher longer."

In throwing the change-up, our Dodger pitchers combined three different methods. They held the ball with three fingers across the seams, used a dead rear leg, and they were instructed to stiffen and bring their wrist right down. "When I threw my change," explained Don Drysdale, "I tried to think that my wrist was going to hit the dirt I used the four-seam rotation to make the hitter think he was getting a fast ball." Using a stiff wrist, the pitcher pulls down on the ball. The heel of the hand should come down first. The ball is held slightly looser than on the fast ball. As the ball is released, the fingertips are raised slightly.

The palmball change is popular with many pitching coaches. According to Roger Craig, "The ball is placed way back in the palm of the hand, the thumb is placed on a seam, and the four fingers lay down across the ball. The pressure is placed between the thumb and the middle and ring finger where they meet the hand. The fingers just lie on the ball. If the pitcher throws it with three fingers, his little finger is placed along the side of the ball. He simply throws the ball with his palm, as if the pitcher had to fingers at all. The tight grip or pressure with the thumb and the knuckle joint will do this automatically. It will lock the wrist and kill the speed of the ball.

Again, the motion on a change-up should correspond to that used on the fast ball. If he slows up his motion, the pitcher will tip off his pitch and any illusion he is trying to create will be lost.

One of the easiest ways to teach a change-up is to have the pitcher turn it over a little, like a screwball. The ball is released at the last split-second so it will come off the hand between the second and third fingers, as a screwball, but without too much wrist snap. Even though it will not break as much as the screwball, the change of speed makes this pitch effective.

Some pitchers find it effective to lengthen the stride on the change-up. Others like to drag the rear foot, using the dead rear leg method with a letup delivery. They hold their foot on the rubber and do not allow their weight to come through. This will reduce the body motion and help keep the body low.

The change-up can be a terrific pitch, especially in tough situations. The let-up pitch is often effective on 3--2, 3--1, or 2--0 counts. After two strikes, the batters guard the plate a little more closely.

The change-of-pace is difficult for many pitchers to learn. One reason is that the pitcher tries to develop an entirely new pitching style. Instead, he should stay with the same style he uses for his other pitches. This is why the turnover change is one of our favorites.

Throwing off-speed pitches takes practice and courage, working on them until they become natural and effective. Young pitchers must not get discouraged if they do not learn the change-up right away. It takes time to learn.

"Development of the straight change requires a concentrated effort," explained Adams. "I required my pitchers to throw as many as twenty-five to thirty in a row in each practice session." Practicing the off-speed pitch is like the hitter who doesn't like to practice bunting. Most pitchers have a tendency to throw more fast balls in practice than any other pitch.

Doyle Alexander, a master at changing speeds on his pitches, advised: "The best way to change speeds on the ball is to hold the ball differently but throw the ball the same as you would your fast ball. Use the same motion!"

Many big-league pitching coaches believe the secret to throwing an effective change-of-pace is getting the pitching arm up high, so the arm speed cannot be picked up by the hitter. Johnny Podres who pitched for me emphasizes the importance of good arm extension. "If a pitcher drops his elbow," says Podres, "he will have trouble getting the elbow up even with the shoulder and letting the elbow go out first and then pulling down on the ball. By reaching up high and throwing the boll on a downward plane, a pitcher can make it very difficult for hitters to pick up the arm speed. It requires a full extension of the arm and a pulling motion at the end.

Palmball

The palmball is used primarily as an off-speed pitch,

but it is more effective when the pitcher has a good fast ball. Dave Guisti, an outstanding relief pitcher with the Pittsburg Pirates in the 1970s, explained that. "If I throw a palmball, with the same motion and delivery, the/speed is cut down enough to throw their timing off. Essentially, that is the key to the success of the palmball." Some major league pitchers prefer the palmball for their change-of-pace. On the palmball, key pressure is applied by the inside joint of the thumb. The four fingers lie gently and slightly curved around the ball. The ball is stuffed into the palm of the hand. The pitcher releases the ball with a fast ball motion by letting it float out of the palm of the hand, controlled by the pressure of his thumb joint

"I hold the ball in the palm of my hand with the pressure points being in the middle of the ring finger, and the middle of the thumb," said Guisti. "In throwing the palmball, I try to minimize the speed with the same motion and delivery. The old cliche, "pulling the window shade down," is true because you have to get the elbow out and use a stiff wrist, You simply try to cut down the speed and the spin. Cutting down on the spin sometimes will affect the pitch similar to a knuckleball and it will sink. We try not to break my wrist very much. The delivery and follow-through have to appear the same as a fast ball; otherwise, the hitters will pick it up."

Unfortunately, the palmball can be hard on the arm. Guisti started throwing the pitch while in college and according to Dave, "It did irritate my elbow to a degree.

Slider

The slider can be a highly effective pitch and has

attained considerable prominence among present-day, major league pitchers. Since it is usually accompanied by a hard snap of the arm, the slider must be thrown properly, so as not to hurt the arm. The stiff wrist slider will cause elbow problems.

Since it is easy to learn and control, many young pitchers in pro ball are throwing it. The curve ball takes longer to master and is more difficult to control. Since the slider does not break as much, the pitcher can put the ball where he wants it.

The slider is held off-center a little, with the middle and index fingers placed to the outside of the ball. If he throws a with-the-seams fast ball, the pitcher might slide 'up' the ball just a little and hold it slightly off-center. The release of the slider can be compared with the passing of a football. Using a good wrist snap through the release area, the pitcher will cut the ball and impart this tight spin. He should think of the power finger, usually the middle finger, as a knife that will slice part of the ball as it is released.

The index finger controls the release. Just before the point of release, the hand should be turned sideways, providing the football spin. Come straight down hard and let the ball come off the second finger. This will cause the ball to spin like a bullet.

The stiff-wrist slider that is taught throughout baseball is the one that will most definitely cause elbow problems. The hand, in this method, comes through the release area as if the pitcher were throwing a football. "With this hand position, the wrist cannot snap or propel the ball forward," explained Bob Cluck. "From this locked position, there is too much pressure on the elbow joint. The pitcher also has a tendency to twist his wrist at the end which places additional strain on the elbow."

To prevent arm trouble, a growing number of coaches are advocating a loose wrist for the slider. With a limber wrist, the pitcher should cut directly through the ball with his middle and index fingers, ending up with a smooth follow-through.

A slider is good when thrown to certain spots, breaking in and jamming a left-handed hitter or clipping the outside corner. It is also effective when thrown so it breaks outside to a right-handed hitter with the hitter reaching for it. But the thing that makes it especially effective is its velocity. It is a fast ball with a break, and should be kept down.

The general feeling among pitching authorities is that the young pitcher should stay away from the slider until he is physically equipped and has sufficient talent to throw it properly.

Sinker

The sinker is one of the greatest weapons of the relief pitcher, particularly those who throw sidearm. With many of the hitters today swinging for the fences, the sinker pitch has been most effective in making the batter hit the ball in the ground. With the correct motion and sinking rotation, the sinker can be a real "bread-and-butter pitch".

Many of the game's top relief pitchers, including Greg Minton, rely heavily on the sinker pitch. Minton developed his sinker ball when a knee injury forced him to cut down on the kick and shorten his stride. The shorter stride has caused him to hasten his arm's downward plunge, adding the type of spin necessary for a good sinker.

Two popular sinker ball grips used by the Dodgers are:

1. Having the fingers close together along the two small seams of the ball.
2. Having the fingers go across the two small seams of the ball.

We also emphasize having the fingers close together and overloading the ball on the inside part, with most of the ball showing on the outside part. The left-handed pitcher releases the ball from the outside part of his hand.

Prior to release, the turn of the arm is more important than is the flip of the wrist. There is a little rotation of the wrist, not really turning the ball over as much as putting more pressure on the forefinger and getting proper rotation. The arm movement sweeping across the pitcher's body gives the sinker a downward rotation. The pitch is released off the right corner tip of the middle finger. The pitcher must stay on top of the ball until the actual point of release.

The sinker should be kept low for maximum effectiveness. Concentrate on keeping the ball from above the knees to below the knees. The thumb plays an important roll in the sinker, as it does in all pitches. The ball can be off-centered by moving the thumb up the side where the little finger is.

There are two types of sinker ball pitchers. First, there is the gifted moundsman, usually with a three-quarter to sidearm delivery, whose delivery makes possible a natural sinker. He is the hard-throwing pitcher who can get on top of the ball to the extent that he does not let it go until it is well out in front of him. He manages to cut the ball just enough in his natural motion so that it will come in and sink.

Then, there is the less gifted pitcher who has to give the ball considerable help when he is releasing it. By bringing his arm clear across the body, he cuts the ball, giving it the necessary reverse corkscrew spin to make it break downward.

The success of the sinker pitch depends on the following coaching points:

1. Hold the ball slightly off-center.
2. Execute the drop-and-go" body movement.
3. Stay on top of the ball.
4. Release the ball off the side of the middle finger, well out in front of the body.
5. Use a sweeping arm action across the body, which cuts the ball at the last moment.

In throwing a good sinker, the pitcher must utilize a body action that drives him toward the hitter in a lower position than his fast ball and his other pitches. The "drop-and-go" movement allows him to stay on top of the ball, cutting and releasing it at the last moment, well out in front of his body.

Bending the right knee causes the body to drop down and then be pushed forward, a "drop-and-go" movement. The throwing arm is extended across the body, finishing up completely across the body. Most pitches lengthen their stride as much as six inches more than on the fast ball. The sinker pitch is just like a fast ball, except that the pitcher brings his arm on across his body. This gives a reverse corkscrew spin to the ball. There is a similarity between the sinker and the screwball, although the screwball is much more taxing on the arm. The sinker is thrown harder than the screwball. The screwball is about a half-speed pitch, which is thrown by actually turning the elbow and arm completely over.

Caution should be taken by the young pitcher, in throwing either of these pitches, in not trying to get too much of an inward arm turn. Too much rotation of the wrist or arm can cause injury to the elbow area.

Screwball

Thrown with an inside-out twist of the hand and wrist, the screwball breaks the opposite way from the curve. A screwball is a reverse curve--a curve breaking away from instead of into a right-handed hitter when thrown by a left-hander. Carl Hubbell, who struck out Babe Ruth and four other future Hall of Famers, explained that "It isn't the way a screwball breaks that bothers a good hitter--it's the change of speed on the screwball compared to a fast ball." Carl got them all on screwballs after setting them up with fast balls and an occasional curve.

The screwball can be a particularly effective pitch for a left-handed pitcher, as the success of Fernando Valenzuela has proven. Yet, it is a difficult pitch to master and is considered by many pitching authorities to be hard on a young arm. Very definitely, some discretion should be shown in throwing the screwball. The clockwise or inward rotation of the arm is unnatural and places undue strain on the arm. This is the prime reason why coaches and managers do not encourage this difficult pitch by young and inexperienced pitchers.

"Most pitchers don't have what it takes, anatomically, to throw a screwball," said Ron Perranoski, pitching coach of the Dodgers. "You've got to have a certain kind of delivery. It is a very difficult pitch to learn. A screwball is thrown with an elongated arc, with great arm extension--almost over your head--and Fernando does that. A pitcher also has to be real loose in all the joints. Most pitchers are not loose-jointed enough to throw it--they can't get the wrist turned over. The action of the arm and wrist as you come over the top, putting spin on the ball, is what makes it break. Valenzuela throws his screwball so effortlessly. He doesn't use the elbow at all."

A good screwball requires more of an overhand delivery, so that the pitcher is on top of the ball. The principle of the pitch is getting the ball to rotate, for a left-handed pitcher, getting the ball to rotate like a right-hand curve ball. It is spun out of the hand between the middle and ring fingers and is given its rotation by the reverse quarter-turn of the wrist and the middle finger release. The thumb is used to increase the reverse spin by being given a last-second flip as the ball is released. We emphasize turning the hand and wrist away from the body and then trying to turn the ball over to get the proper rotation.

Jim Brewer, a former relief pitcher on our club who can attribute much of his success to the screwball, explained that: "The screwball has not been hard on my arm because I extend my arm, and I am not using the elbow. From time to time, I have had a problem with my shoulder, but it has not been serious. It is just a tight muscle from throwing the screwball too much."

"When a young pitcher starts to throw a screwball," continued Brewer, "they must not try to throw it too hard. They should get the feel of it and see that it is rotating properly. As they learn more about the rotation and how to throw it, they can begin to throw it hard. I would not advise them to throw more than one or two screwballs out of six pitches."

The screwball is generally gripped along the long seam providing a four-seam rotation. As the arm comes forward, the pitcher should think fast ball until the last instant, then rotate the hand and release the fingers over the top of the ball. The thumb plays a major role in imparting the clockwise rotation to the ball. Screwball pitchers often develop blisters on the top side of their thumbs because of the pressure exerted on the ball.

The split-finger fast ball and the forkball are almost the same, but the reason a growing number of pitching coaches are calling this pitch a split-finger fast ball is because the "fast ball" is the key word. As the pitcher spreads his fingers apart and moves into his delivery, he should be thinking in the back of his mind, "I am throwing a fast ball."

"The way I teach this Ditch is to have the pitcher throw a fast ball and gradually work the fingers down on the seams until it feels comfortable to grip the ball between the two fingers," explained Roger Craig, veteran pitching coach of the Detroit Tigers. "You simply spread the fingers apart and throw a fast ball.

You get the arm speed of a fast ball, yet you have the baseball speed of a change-up. Once you practice this pitch and throw it quite a bit, the ball really starts to do tricks. Most of the time it breaks down. It's like an off-speed pitch and is very easy on the arm and easy to learn, too. It's a great pitch and gets a lot of outs!"

"Hold the ball with the seams and throw a fast ball," said Craig. "Next time, open up another half an inch and throw another fastball and gradually keep working down until the grip feels comfortable. Some pitchers who have a deep thumb hold it a third of the way down, while some a fourth of the way, but it has to work out best for each individual."

"The secret to throwing a split-finger fast ball is when you get down as far as you want to go, halfway down, or whatever, you have to think that you are throwing a fast ball. This is what deceives a hitter because the arm speed comes through like a fast ball. When I see my pitchers letting up on their motion, I tell them to think 'fast ball.' Even if the ball goes straight, you still have a great off-speed pitch."

The release point is almost identical to the fast ball. The pitcher should make sure he pulls the fingers through the ball. "You get the feeling that you are throwing through the ball," said Roger. "In releasing the ball, you have to give the pitch a lot of wrist like you are throwing a fast ball. The ball has to come out between the two fingers."

Bruce Sutter holds his thumb on the side of the baseball. He pushes in on the ball and gives it a "thumbing effect." Other pitchers may have the thumb underneath or halfway down.

As a major league pitcher, Craig never threw forkball, but now, all but a few of his Detroit pitchers can throw it and most of them pretty effectively. Jack Morris gets 50% of his outs using this pitch. Craig explained, "It all started when I had the school with Little League pitchers in San Diego. When young pitchers have only one type of pitch, a fast ball, they want something else, and if you don't teach them something that won't hurt their arms, they'll learn something on their own and only hurt themselves. I advised some of the young pitchers to spread the fingers out in some form of forkball and throw a regular fast ball.

After talking to many doctors and orthopedic surgeons, I am convinced that the split-finger fast ball is a very good pitch for young pitchers because there is no strain or added tension in the arm. Some pitchers who throw the forkball for the first time make the mistake of throwing it with a stiff wrist. This places considerable strain on the elbow, much the same as the "locked" wrist slider.

Knuckleball

The knuckler is the Most Popular of the unorthodox deliveries and has been used with great success by such modern-day hurlers as Hoyt Wilhelm, Phil and Joe Niekro. The name of the pitch, in most cases, is a misnomer because the knuckleball is actually thrown with the fingernails. The publicity this pitch has received is probably due to the difficulty catchers have in catching it. The knuckler probably takes the most erratic course to the plate of any type pitch. Its movement is highly unpredictable. It may sink, swerve to either side, or jump in a crazy manner. It is not only a difficult pitch for the pitcher to control, but is easy to run on. Since this pitch is just about impossible to hide, the success of the knuckleball is due to its action rather than to the surprise element.

There are several methods used in throwing the knuckleball. The method favored by most pitchers is to dig the fingernails into the seams. On release, the fingers are extended vigorously and push the ball toward the plate. While the fingernail pitch can be thrown with one, two, or three fingers, most pitchers use the two-finger method. In this technique, the finger and wrist remain stiff. The ball rarely revolves when thrown in this manner. The other method is to hold the ball cradled against the first joints of the fingers. The first joints of the index and middle fingers rest against the ball between the seams where they are narrowest. The thumb and fourth and fifth fingers encircle the ball and hold it tightly. As the ball leaves the throwing hand, the bent fingers are extended, giving the pitch additional speed. This method requires a good amount of wrist snap as the ball leaves the hand, plus the extension of the index and middle fingers. The result is that the ball revolves only slightly.

The floater or butterfly type of knuckleball is thrown at half-speed, with a stiff wrist. As it approaches the plate, it seems to dance, reacting to each shift in air currents.

Conversely, the fast knuckler is thrown at full speed. The fingers are extended as the ball is released and the wrist snapped, giving the bail extra velocity and sufficient downspin to make it dip sharply as it approaches the hitter, like "rolling off the table."

Certainly, the knuckleball is not recommended for pitchers in high school or lower age levels. The pitch is difficult to control and development of the pitch usually takes years.

Basic 20 of Pitching

1. Be consistent in your windup.
2. Keep the ball hidden throughout the delivery.
3. Make a good pivot, keeping the foot parallel to the rubber.
4. Retain your weight during the pivot.
5. Use your hips properly--activate them!
6. Have a well balanced leg lift--don't start the kick too soon.
7. Keep your eyes fixed on the target--concentrate!
8. Keep the ball in the glove longer.
9. Drive off from the rubber--get a good thrust!
10. Drop and drive right out at the hitter.
11. Open up the stride and unlock the hips--don't throw across the body.
12. Do not overstride or rush the stride.
13. Utilize good arm extension by getting the pitching arm up high and elbow out in front.
14. Have good rhythm--put it all together!
15. Use strong wrist and arm action.
16. Throw strikes--stay ahead of the hitter.

17. Be quick with the top part of your body--whip the arm through!

18. Use a comfortable and natural arm angle.

19. Create a consistent point of release.

20. Follow-through in a natural manner.

The delivery

All successful pitchers throw the ball in the way that is easiest and most effective for them. Proper form and delivery are different for each pitcher. Therefore, each pitcher should be able to work out his own natural style. A good pitching delivery is one that seems to flow in a smooth, full-arm swing, finishing with a powerful snap of the wrist. On the other hand, a half-swing, bent arm, jerky motion will likely place undue stress on the elbow and may ruin the pitching arm permanently.

A well-coordinated and rhythmic delivery will provide extra speed and power, and help the pitcher achieve better control. Rather than just the arm, every part of the body will bear the brunt of the effort. There are four basic types of pitching delivery: overhand, three-quarter, sidearm, and underhand. Normally, most pitchers throw overhand or three-quarter style, adding an occasional sidearm pitch. It is the angle of delivery that makes the several styles different.

No matter what style is used, there are certain basic qualities which are absolutely essential. In any type of delivery, the pitcher must have balance, a proper pivot, correct stride, and a good follow-through. Practice will give him the coordination and rhythm needed for an effective pitching delivery.

Regardless of which delivery is used, every pitch must be thrown with about the same motion and released from almost the same point. If the pitcher throws his fast ball sidearm and curve ball overhand, the batter obviously will be able to detect what is being thrown.

In pitching, everything has to work together. The throwing arm and upper body must be meshed with the striding leg and lower body. If the striding loot hits arm is way back, all a pitcher has is a pulling motion. In this case, the leg stride is too quick or the upper body and pitching arm is too slow. The problem is that the upper half of the body trails the lower half.

The solution is to: 1) slow down the stride and 2) speed up the arm and upper body. By slowing down the stride, the pitcher give his throwing arm a chance to get through at the right time.

How can proper rhythm and timing be achieved? How can a pitcher generate an action of power?

1. Keep the ball in the glove a little longer. By keeping the ball in the glove longer, the pitcher holds up the thrust of the lower part of his body.
2. Do not start the leg kick too soon or employ a higher kick. Delaying the stride will prevent rushing.
3. Open up the stride and unlock the hips. Give the throwing arm and upper body the opportunity to shoot through.
4. Get the pitching arm on top and drive on through. The pitcher must get up on top before the lead foot hits.

5. Whip the arm through. The pitcher should be exceptionally quick with the top part of his body. He cannot be lazy with his arm.

Getting the sign

While standing on the mound, the pitcher should keep the ball hidden from the hitter's view. Most pitchers today have the ball in the glove just in front of their waist line. Others have a practice of hiding the pitching hand and ball behind the thigh of their pivot leg. The less the hitter sees of the ball, the better it is for the pitcher. To take the signal from the catcher, the pitcher must stand on the rubber. In fact, the rules require this. He is also required to deliver the ball to the batter within twenty seconds after he receives the signal.

The majority of pitchers place their pivot foot on the rubber and their other foot a comfortable distance behind it. The spikes of the pivot foot are over the front of the rubber, with the striking foot behind and just to the left.

Occasionally the pitcher might shake off several of the catcher's signals until he comes back a second time to the pitch he really wants to throw. This makes the hitter think and wonder about pitches the pitcher may not even have.

Windup

The primary purpose of the windup is to move the body weight back in order to place power into the pitch. To transfer the body weight effectively to the push-off foot, many pitchers will take an initial step back on the striding foot. In preparing for the start of the windup, the pitcher should "gather his weight" in order to get more power into his delivery. This pattern of action resembles that of a pendulum. By reaching way back, the pitcher will have necessary explosive charge to propel the ball toward the plate. The main thing in starting a windup is to be consistent. As the arms swing forward and upward to a comfortable position above the head, the ball should be hidden in the glove well up into the web, so that the pitching hand is hidden by the glove. This action conceals the ball so that the batter cannot see the grip and know what is coming. When the pitcher makes his pivot, the ball remains hidden behind the glove and then his body. As a result, the batter does not see the ball until it is coming toward him. Most pitching instructors instruct their pitchers to pitch "out of their glove," as opposed to "out of their hand."

To go into this motion more effectively, the pitcher should place the front his pivot foot over the edge of the rubber. By angling his foot slightly toward the side from which he will throw, he facilitates the pivot and gets his body weight behind the throw. In fact, the pitcher will be more effective by keeping his foot in front of the rubber, rather than on top of it.

Although almost all major league pitchers have eliminated the backward swing pumping action, young pitchers may find they have better rhythm using the pumping action. The purpose of the pump is to loosen and relax the arm and letting the arms swing backward, with the wrists flexing.

Movement of hands: Most pitchers today move their hands, the throwing hand inside the glove hand, to an area in front of or on top of the head, or to the side. When moving the all and glove up with this hands, the pitcher should make certain they do not block his view.

Hiding the ball The back of the glove should always face the hitter, and the ball should be up in the webbing, not in the heel of the glove. The ball and the pitching hand down to the wrist should be wrapped inside the glove.

Perhaps the most significant change in pitching technique during the past two decades has been the switch from the full windup with a pumping motion to the no-pump windup that every pitcher uses today. Until the early 1970s, both arms hung loosely down to the pitcher's sides, and the pitcher would then begin his preliminary pumping motions.

Today, the pitcher's hands are together in front of the body when he starts his delivery. As the hands come up and over his head, the right-handed pitcher steps back with the left foot. He then shifts his weight forward as he rotates into the pitch. A more compact delivery and good balance are the two chief benefits of the no-pump windup.

The start of the delivery should be as short and comfortable as possible. The important thing is to stay compact and not waste any motion. The arms should not be flailing around.

Position of the hands The hands are held immediately in front of the waist, with the pitching hand grasping the ball inside the glove.

Stance The pitcher starts his delivery with both feet on the rubber. As he faces the hitter, the pitcher's feet are nearly square on the rubber.

Rock-back Most pitchers take a step, either back or to the side, in order to get the momentum moving. After stepping back or to the side, the pitcher then brings the leg up.

Pivot

A good pivot is essential to an effective pitching delivery. If he fails to pivot correctly, very likely the pitcher will be throwing with just his arm, and he will lack the necessary balance. As the pitcher's arms come up over his head during the windup, his weight should shift back on his rear foot. For proper balance, his pivot foot must be placed comfortably in contact with the rubber as it is turned.

The actual pivoting is executed without lifting the foot from the rubber. It is performed on the ball of the foot, and when completed, the toe points in the direction of third. This maneuver is very important, in that it makes possible the extreme body pivot to the right and back.

At the start of the pivot, the pitcher's stance should be slightly open, with the toe of his pivot foot pointed out slightly toward third base (for a right-hander). Pivoting on the ball of his right foot, he turns his pivot foot parallel to the rubber. Keeping the ball hidden from the hitter's view, he pivots his body around and exposes his rear to the hitter. His eyes remain focused on the target.

As the pivot takes place, the pitcher brings the knee of his free foot up high across the body as the arms swing down and back. This leg action bends and pivots the body backward.

The important thing on the pivot is proper balance--with the weight of the body over the pivot leg, which is slightly bent at the knee. The body should not be leaning forward. Some pitchers have their bodies moving forward during their pivot, and actually start their kick while their pitching arm is still going down and back. The result will be the arm working all alone in the pitch.

Many young pitchers get very little kick in their delivery, because they start their body moving forward before the pivot is completed. Instead, they might take a slight pause, like Seaver, to make sure they have everything together, before they proceed. This will slow them down enough to get their balance and timing together before they throw to the plate.

Weight retention

A pitcher has to retain his weight during the pivot and wait for his arm to come though. Weight retention, on which Red Adams placed so much stress with his pitchers, means, "Don't run off and leave the arm." If he runs off and leaves his arm, of course, the pitcher will not have time to get his arm up on top, and he will have to shorten up somehow. This could cause him to "shortarm the ball" or throw sidearm. Waiting until the hands get completely to the top lessens the chance of rushing.

Rushing is the most serious mechanical problem with which pitching instructors must deal. The team "rushing" applies to the body getting ahead of the arm. It is a problem of timing and coordination. If the pitching arm is not up, back, and extended when the stride foot is planted, the pitcher will likely rush his delivery. To retain their weight during the pivot, pitchers should practice a slower delivery than normal while warming up. Many pitching coaches emphasize a slow, deliberate "lifting" of the free leg and a smooth, effortless stride.

Leg kick

To obtain good forward drive, the overhand pitcher should bring the knee of his free foot up high across the body as the arms swing down and back. This leg action bends and pivots the body backward, and as the pitcher strides forward with the striding foot, the entire body goes into the pitch like an uncoiling spring, providing maximum power. Many different types of leg lifts are used by pitchers, depending on their style of delivery. The pitcher with an overhand, erect type of delivery cannot effectively turn his back to the hitter during the pivot, as it creates a horizontal type body action. However, the turning of the back to the hitter is very effective for the coiling, three-quarter or sidearm type pitcher.

A pitcher must execute a well-balanced leg kick with good body control. His weight is more on the ball of his right foot as he pivots into the backswing. He now has the balance necessary for a good thrust forward from the rubber.

As the leg lift takes place, three key points should be kept in mind:

1. The pitcher's body should be twisted back as far as possible without ruining balance.
2. His eyes should remain fixed on home plate or the target. A pitcher should look over his left shoulder as he swings back.
3. The pitching arm should drop well down behind his body and be straightened out.

At this point, the right leg should be similar to a coiled spring. Uncoiling is the movement that pushes the pitcher into the actual pitch, generating drive into the motion. The size of the leg kick varies with the individual pitcher. However, he should not kick so high that it ruins his balance, overall coordination and control. For some pitchers, a, high leg kick is a big asset because it gives them a deceptive motion and a high angle of delivery. The leg kick gives the hitter more motion at which to look and tends to bother his timing. Unquestionably, Juan Marichal's famous high kick was a prime factor in his outstanding success.

Not every pitcher, though, feels he is properly balanced with the extra-high leg kick. Each pitcher must experiment until he feels his delivery is smooth and coordinated and has the balance necessary for the push-off forward. While the deceptiveness of a high kick helps hide the ball longer from the batter, the pitcher should never sacrifice balance for deception.

Hip rotation

Proper hip action is probably the greatest single factor involved in a powerful As in batting, the hips generate a great amount of power. While a good push-off from the rubber is essential, correct use of the hips is perhaps the prerequisite for a powerful thrust from the slab. With the weight on the pivot foot, the hips are rotated to the right. The knee free foot is brought up high across the body as the arms swing down and back. The pitcher's eyes are kept on the target throughout the delivery. The action of the hips is bolstered by driving the rear knee down as the hips are opened and the stride is completed.

"I like to see a pitcher use his hips as much as he can in lifting his leg," said Red Adams. "If a fellow will lift his leg and bring his knee back a little toward second base this will throw the bottom of his foot a little bit out toward home plate. This will activate his hips, and put his hips on a slight tilt. Of course, when he comes on through, it gives him some good leg action and momentum."

"Good hip action comes from the way a pitcher raises his knee. The belt line is the key to watch for. If the belt is on a level plane during his pivot, generally his legs and hips are not activated like they could be. If they are tilted a little, the chances are he has the desired hip action."

Thrust

By bending the knee of his pivot leg, the pitcher lowers his body, thus getting a better position to drive off--to thrust out! This forces the pitcher to put extra effort into his pitch. When he drops and bends his knee in order to get the necessary momentum, he has to drive off the rubber. A pitcher must not pitch from a lazy pivot leg. This leg should be bent in order to get balance and a good thrust forward. Pitchers who are in poor condition or just plain lazy are more apt to pitch from a stiff or dead pivot leg.

Some pitching authorities, like Bob Cluck, believe the back leg does not drive the pitcher to the plate. Bob explains that, "the 'push' is merely the violent rotation of the hips and shoulders as they open up. This momentum will pull (often explosively) the back side through and bring the rear leg forward."

Seaver is a good example of a pitcher who users

the "drop-and-drive" technique. He pitchers between his hips, keeping his body weight as close under the hips as possible. He drives low and right out at the hitter. When Tom drops and drives, his right knee is dirty from hitting the ground. As the pitcher pushes forward off his pivot foot, the entire body goes into the pitch like an uncoiling spring, providing maximum power and drive.

The pitcher who thrusts out too quickly with the lower part of his body can hold up the thrust by keeping the ball in his glove longer. He might exaggerate keeping the ball in the glove until the upper half of his body is ready for thrust. Otherwise, the lower part starts too soon--it gets a head Start. Young pitchers often hurry their deliveries by taking the ball out of the too soon. When the glove goes, the foot goes. Therefore, the young pitcher should delay the stride by keeping the ball in the glove, a little longer.

While dropping low has been used effectively by many pitchers through the years, it should be remembered that there is a certain advantage in throwing from a more upright position. The flight of the ball, or trajectory, is at a great angle. As the pitcher steps to throw, it is important for him to step almost straight forward with his striding foot. This step will eliminate any possibility of throwing across the body. The stride should be comfortable and natural. The stride is simply a step in the direction of home plate and is not a power movement. Pitchers who use the stride as a power movement will rush their delivery and experience the problem of overstriding.

The length of the stride depends on a pitcher's

height and how it suits his size and comfort. Most important, he should guard against overstriding, one of the chief faults in pitching technique. Generally, if the stride is too straight, too long, or too far crossed-over, the pitcher will have a tendency to pitch high as well as outside.

A pitcher can open up the stride and get his arm on top by moving his lead foot over. A straight overarm pitcher has to open up his stride more. To make sure that he does no* throw against his body and that his hips are opened fully, the pitcher's stride foot should land on, or to the first base side of, an imaginary line drawn toward the plate from between the pitcher's feet. Many coaches will draw this line in the dirt with a bat.

The stride should be completed before the pitcher has reached the top point of his delivery. His left foot and leg should be planted firmly in the dirt before he starts to apply the genuine power of the pitch. In other words, he is pitching against the anchor of his left leg which braces his body.

One of the key points in the stride and follow-through is that the knee of the pitcher's striding leg should remain bent to avoid jarring. This bent knee should be flexible so that it will give with the pitch and enable the pitcher to obtain the type of follow-through necessary for speed and control.

The toe and heel should strike the ground almost simultaneously, although the ball of the foot should take most of the shock. The pitcher's toe should be pointed toward the plate. It is important that he step in the same spot for each pitch.

A pitcher must not rush the stride. He should not rush out with the bottom half of his body. The average pitcher tends to move the lower part of his body ahead too quickly. He wants to start kicking too soon. His leg stride is too quick.

To counteract a tendency to thrust out too quickly, pitchers such as Sandy Koufax, Warren Spahn, and Juan Marichal used a higher leg kick. The leg lift not only gets drive into the motion, but gives the arm movement more time to get on top of the pitch.

Arm angle

Every pitcher has an angle of delivery from which his fast ball is most effective. A change in speed and velocity can be detected by lowering or raising the arm angle even a few inches. The arm angle for most pitchers varies from low three-quarters to high three-quarters. A high three-quarters is more desirable, since it provides a downward plane and is particularly complimentary to the curve ball.

A pitcher can lose a considerable amount of spin and action on the fast ball because of a poor angle and impairment of natural coordination. Therefore, it is important for the coach to find the best angle of delivery for each of his pitchers. The three-quarter overhand delivery is the most natural one for the majority of pitchers.

Essentially, every pitch should be thrown from the same angle, so that the pitcher will not tip his pitches. If he throws his fast ball sidearm and his curve overhand, the hitter will soon know what is coming. Occasionally, however, a pitcher might want to lower the angle of his delivery, even coming around from

Port Arthur, that is, stepping toward the third-base line and cross-firing past a right-handed hitter.

Arm and wrist action

The arm action of a pitcher should be a smooth, free movement with little muscular tension. His arm should be loose and relaxed as it swings backward in the windup. He should start to cock his arm as soon as his body begins to move forward again.

A pitcher's throwing arm should be away from his body, so he can bring the ball back and throw it in one continuous motion. The arm works as a unit with the back and shoulder. When the arm starts forward, the wrist should bend back. Then the elbow comes through, followed by the forward action of the arm and wrist. The arm should be up high. The elbow should not be below the shoulder and should precede his wrist as it comes past his shoulder point. The muscles of the pitcher's hand and wrist must be relaxed prior to the release, so that a maximum wrist snap will take place. Keeping his arm loose, the pitcher should snap it forward like a whip as he makes his throw. The release of the ball should be off the first two fingers, with a downward snap of the wrist. A strong wrist action will impart a spin to the ball, which accompanied by speed, causes it to hop as it is affected by air currents.

Pitching on a downward plane

A major factor in pitching success is the pitcher's ability to throw the ball on a downward plane. Many of the pitching greats of baseball utilized high arm angles, with the point of release high above the ear. The greater the angle downward, the greater the advantage to the pitcher, is a principle that pitching coach Ray Berres for years successfully employed with the Chicago White Sox. Berres was a stickler for the correct execution of the proper mechanics of pitching, particularly the arm angle and downward plane. Pitching on a downward plane means that the ball is moving in two planes, forward and down. The hitter, generally, swings the bat parallel to the ground, in a single plane. When the ball is released above the ear, it follows a downward trajectory which can cause the hitter difficulty in making solid contact.

The elbow must be up, at shoulder level or above. "If a pitch is made with a dropped elbow, the pitcher's hand will be traveling almost parallel to the ground," explained Bob Shaw, former pitching star of the Chicago White Sox. "As a result, he cannot pitch on a downward plane." While a high arm angle and overhand delivery are mechanically desirable, a pitcher should use a style of his own and throw naturally. The arm angle should be one that feels most comfortable and natural.

Release

The most effort employed in the pitching delivery comes when the pitcher is actually releasing and unloading the ball. Everything before is preparation. Proper release is essential for good control, maximum spin, and smooth follow-through. It is wrist action and the release of the ball that are most responsible for imparting good stuff on the pitch.

The arm and wrist are loose and relaxed as the ball is released with good wrist snap. The index and middle fingers pull downward on the ball to make sure that the ball will have plenty of spin.

Although the actual release point is above and in front of the head, the pitcher must think about releasing the ball well out in front of him to achieve maximum effectiveness. In other words, he must think low when releasing the ball. After coming over the top, he must release the ball with his fingers on top of the ball, imparting strong wrist action. The pitcher tries to create a consistent point of release, just as the golfer tries to create a consistent point of contact. By throwing the ball over and over, the pitcher will be able to find the correct release point. He can tell by feel that he is releasing the ball correctly.

If he opens up too soon, he will release too quickly. The front arm and shoulder will be too far forward, and the throwing arm will be too far in back of the body. This type of action will result in poor control and wear and tear on the body.

Follow-through

A good follow-through is important for speed, control, and a proper fielding position. A pitching motion that stops abruptly upon release of the ball hinders the speed and control of the pitch. The pitcher's arm should snap straight across his chest to his left knee, with the pivot foot swinging around to a position almost parallel to his striding foot. His left leg and foot must remain firmly planted, because pitching against the resistance of the right leg gives the pitch its final snap.

The pitcher's eyes should be on the target, his back bent, and his weight evenly distributed, with the knees slightly bent. His glove should be brought up in front of his body so that he is in good fielding position.

However, there are pitchers who really whip the pitch. Consequently, they often end up in poor fielding positions. Rather than change their natural delivery, it is often best to teach them to make adjustments after completing the pitch, such as getting the feet parallel and ready to move in either direction. Any move which might curtail their motion and deception should be carefully considered. A number of big-league pitching coaches believe the follow-through is overrated. They cite a number of successful pitchers who stand up straight and fail to complete the weight transfer on their pitches.

Control

Good location of pitches is essential for pitching success. A pitcher may have overwhelming stuff, but unless he can locate his pitches, he will not be effective. I have always figured that if a pitcher puts the all over the plate, he will give up some home runs, but a solo homer is a lot better than a three-run homer, which is what he's liable to give up if he walks people.

The main thing in pitching is to get the ball over the plate with good stuff on it, and be able to get the breaking pitches over. Control is the big difference between a thrower and a pitcher. The pitcher rarely walks anybody and hits those corners much of the time. When he wants to keep the ball clown, he can keep it down. For good control, a pitcher must be in a groove. He must be mechanically the same. Every pitch must mean something, whether he is throwing in the bullpen, throwing batting practice, or throwing in a game itself. He must concentrate and keep his eyes continually on a target.

The mental factor is often the chief reason for poor control. Many pitchers do not concentrate enough on what they are trying to do. Mentally, they have to feel they can get the ball into the strike zone. So, they must "think the ball over the plate." According to many pitching authorities, low pitching is the secret of successful pitching, because if a ball is down, batters tend to hit the ball into the ground more than they do if it is up in the air. When it is on the ground, some fielder has a chance to catch it.

If a pitcher lacks the necessary control, he should not consider pitching in and out, high and low, or everything low. Instead of throwing to spots, he should aim for the middle of the plate and hope his natural stuff takes care of the corners. Although good control involves the ability to throw strikes, there are times when the pitcher should throw a ball, like when setting up the next pitch.

Most pitchers prefer throwing to the glove in the middle of the body. This is the target that enables the pitcher to split the catcher. After giving the signal, therefore, the catcher should move slightly into that area, slightly inside or slightly outside and give his target. The pitcher should divide the strike zone into possibly six areas and go for an area, rather than smaller, more difficult to hit spots.

Wildness often comes from a poor stride, either over or understriding. Landing on the heel, aiming the ball, and taking the eyes off the target are all causes of poor control. Good control takes practice--considerable practice. The pitcher must be sure his grip is correct, that his delivery is the same each time. He must not pitch across his body, "Most important, the release point should be the same," said Adams. "He shouldn't release it here one time and down there another time." Pitchers should throw from a mound at all times. Throwing or warming-up from flat ground is one way of throwing the pitcher out of his groove or pattern.

The following points are essential for achieving good control:

1. Do not go into your windup without thinking where you are going to pitch the ball.
2. Keep your eye on the target and concentrate on the spot the catcher is giving you.
3. Make sure your catcher is always in a squatting position, and that will make you, pitch low.
4. There are four pitching targets: the catcher's knees and his shoulders. Keep your eye on one of these targets during the entire motion.
5. Watch your front foot, where you place your front foot down, and make sure it always lands on the same spot.
6. Make certain you let the ball go only when your arm is in front of you. If you find that your pitches are too high, chances are you are releasing the ball too soon.
7. Be sure you follow through across your body.
8. Keep ahead of the hitter. Make that first pitch a strike!

Proper mental attitude

A pitcher's frame of mind is of great importance to his overall performance, particularly his control. Confidence and poise, when blended with a strong competitive spirit, can be a huge asset to any pitcher. He has to feel he has everything completely under control. He must fell deep down that he is better than the hitter. He has to think positively that "I am going to do it!" "I never pitch a game that I do not expect to win," said Seaver. "I think positively."

The pitcher has to have courage to throw the ball into he strike zone and has to be confident that he has the pitches and control to retire any hitter. Relaxation is of vital importance in acquiring a good mental attitude. Whenever there is fear in the mind of a pitcher, there is tension, and that means he is not relaxed.

Here is how a pitcher can relax:

1. Concentrate on the exact spot you are going to throw the pitch.
2. Take a deep breath before making your pitch.
3. Do not be afraid you are going to walk the hitter.
4. Do not be afraid the batter will get a hit.

A pitcher has a job to do on the mound, and if he places his complete concentration on what lie is doing and how he is going to work on the hitter and get him out, there will be no room for fear in his mind.

Hiding the ball

Every pitcher must work hard on keeping the ball hidden as long as possible. Hiding the ball until the instant it is released gives the batter that much less time to get his eye on it. Many pitchers throw hard, but somehow their pitches come up to the plate big as a balloon. Very likely, their shortcomings can be attributed to a lack of deception and motion. They fail to hide their pitches effectively. The batter is able to pick up the ball early and can follow it all the way. Then, there is the successful pitcher whose motion and deceptiveness are so effective the hitter is prevented from seeing the ball until it is right on him. Consequently, the batter cannot get around in time to pull the trigger.

A pitcher's glove makes a perfect cover-up for the ball as he gets ready to make his delivery. As a result, most pitchers use as large a glove as possible. Many pitchers change the position of their hand on the ball, and the wrist gives the pitch away as much as the fingers on the ball. Consequently, the pitcher should just lay his wrist across the heel of his glove.

How to cover up pitches

1. Wear a large glove that will help cover up the pitches.
2. Hold the ball the same way for all pitches.
3. Start every pitch the same way.
4. Cover the all with the glove at all times.
5. Keep the ball hidden behind the body during the windup.
6. Throw the knee in front of the body.
7. Keep ball in the glove longer--until the last moment.
8. Swing the glove hand toward the hitter.

Distracting the batter

There are various ways of distracting the hitter. Many

pitchers like to swing their gloved hand in front of the throwing hand as they pitch. Certainly, a flick of the glove in the batter's line of vision can prove somewhat annoying. Kicking the leg higher in the air can provide more deception in the delivery. However, caution should be taken not to employ the unorthodox type used by Juan Marichal. Unfortunately, the great majority of pitchers cannot execute this difficult maneuver properly.

Tipping pitches

Many young pitchers tip off their pitches. Some type of movement gives their intentions away. Therefore, the coach should study each of his pitchers closely to determine whether or not he is tipping his pitches. To keep from tipping his pitches, the pitcher should strive to throw every pitch in the same manner. He should hide the ball well up in the web of his glove.

The following is a list of other ways pitchers might be tipping their pitches:

1. Raising the leg higher on one type than on another.
2. Spreading the fingers on certain pitches and not on others.
3. Showing more white on certain pitches.
4. Turning the glove differently when delivering certain pitches.
5. Turning the wrist more on one pitch than another as the pitching hand raises up in the glove.
6. Changing the arm angles on different pitches.

Set position

When there are runners on base, the pitcher should

throw from the set position rather than from a windup position. However, he should use the same pitching procedure from the stretch as he does from a windup. He must not vary his style. Some pitchers are not as effective when working from the set position as they are when using their windup. Quite often, this is because they do not spend enough time throwing from the stretch position on the sidelines. In the set position, the pitcher keeps his feet comfortably spread, his body turned sideways to home plate, with the pivot foot resting against the front edge of the rubber.

Stretching his arms overhead, he brings his hands down to the belt. This is the set position he must come to and hold for at least one full second before throwing to the hitter. He looks at the base runner, and throws to the base, steps off the rubber, or pitches to the batter.

Most pitchers hold their hands at their belts, while some hold them with their arms straight. Others hold them up by their chest. The rear leg should be slightly bent, with most of the weight on it, so that a strong push-off can be made. The right-hander, with a runner on first base, should rotate his shoulders slightly toward first base and turn his head down and toward first so that by moving his eyes he can see both his catcher and the runner on first.

Holding runners on

Since most stolen bases result from the base runner stealing on the pitcher, it is extremely important for all pitchers to develop a good move to first base. As a rule, the more dangerous the base runner, the more often the pitcher must throw over to keep him close to the base.

"Keep the runner honest,' said Spahn. "Let him know you have a deceptive move. His respect for you, will keep him closer to the bag." Quickness and accuracy, not velocity, are the essential factors in all pick-offs, The quicker a pitcher can move his feet and get his upper body into throwing position, the quicker he will be able to release the ball. The pitcher's "unloading time" is a big factor in the success of the base runner. After becoming set, the elapsed time from his first move to release the ball to the plate should be under 1.3 seconds. With concentration and effort, a pitcher can cut his unloading time, but attempts to decrease it too quickly can cause mechanical problems in his delivery.

Before pitching to the batter, many right-handed pitchers make an initial move with their shoulders, arms, body, legs, or feet, but when throwing to first base will always lift the right heel as the starting move. As a result, the base runner will watch the right heel. He will know the pitch is going to the plate if the heel does not lift, thereby getting a good start toward second. The pitcher can remedy the situation by developing the same initial move for the throw to the batter as the one to first base.

With a runner on first base, the right-handed pitcher should use peripheral vision. He should watch the runner out of the corner of his eye. He makes his throw to first by pivoting quickly to the left on his right foot and stepping toward the base with his left foot. The throw to first should be low and to the inside of the base. Quickness is more important than the speed of the throw.

Aggressiveness is essential in any pick-off move.

The pitcher can speed up his action by hopping on his pivot foot as it is turned toward the base. A jump shift, coming down or, the pivot foot first and then on the other foot, is quicker than a pivot.

The best time to throw to, first is when the pitcher comes down to a set position and Just as the runner starts to take his lead. This is particularly true if his first step is a crossover, which places him in a position from which it is difficult to get back to first base quickly. Sometimes, the pitcher likes to pivot and throw when he is at the height of his upswing on the stretch. Or, he might throw when coming down or after coming to a full stop. A pitcher must not fall into a pattern. For example, he should not look at the runner the same number of times or take the same amount of time during and after every stretch. A good base runner will spot it and will be able to get a good jump on him.

A high leg kick with runners on base can also be dangerous. Instead, the kick should be quick, or merely a flat, quick stride. Most pitchers like to employ some type of kick, since it allows them to get more hip action into their delivery. Since he is facing first base, a southpaw pitcher is obviously in a better position to hold the runner on.

Many pitchers do not throw to first base often enough, nor do they vary their timing in throwing to the plate or to first. An effective procedure is to throw to first with medium speed to keep the runner close, and with good speed when trying to pick him off. When holding a runner on second base, the pitcher should take a normal stance, feet parallel, with the toes pointing straight ahead. In making the throw, he uses a jump shift toward the gloved hand side, which is quicker and smoother than turning toward the throwing hand side. With a runner at second, the pitcher might look back toward second base, look toward the plate, look back toward second again out of the corner of his eye to keep the runner honest, then focus on the target and pitch.

All pitchers should be aware that they do not have to complete their throws to either second or third, but that they must in throwing to first. The rules state that, in throwing to first base, the pitcher must step toward the base. Once he moves any part of his body, other than his head, toward first base, the ball must be thrown to first and he must step toward the bag along with the throw. If the runner on first breaks before the pitch, the pitcher should back off the rubber by lifting his divot toot and placing it behind the rubber. He is now out of the box, and cannot commit a balk. He should turn to his left and start toward the runner.

If the runner keeps on going, the throw should be made to second base. If the runner stops halfway, the pitcher should run at him and make him commit himself.

Southpaw pitchers who have a deceptive move to first base have a big advantage in holding runners on base. A basic principle in developing a good move is for the pitcher not to change what he does mechanically to the plate. In throwing to first base, he should duplicate what he does to the plate, at least until the stride leg gets to its highest, point. "If the left-handed pitchers can freeze the runner until point, then the runner can't possibly gain a good jump," explained Bob Cluck. "In achieving this position with the proper deception, they must make their mechanics appear they are going home."

In throwing to first base, the left-hander must step to the left of the 45-degree angle. He should also shorten his arm arc to allow for a quicker release of the ball. Once the pitcher breaks the plane with his right foot, he cannot legally throw to first base but must go to the plate. To prevent a base runner from getting a good jump, a pitcher must try to destroy the runner's timing. An effective tactic is to come to the set position and simply hold the ball for an extended period.

Preventing the balk

Any motion by the pitcher, such as hand or leg movement, turn of the shoulder, that is started, stopped, or in any way interrupted, is a balk. A pitcher always has the option to back off the rubber when he doesn't like what he sees. He must step back with his rear foot. When the pitcher commits a ball, a base runner is allowed to advance to the next base. The following are ways in which the balk can be prevented:

1. The pitcher must have his foot in contact with the rubber when pitching.
2. Once the pitcher has started his motion to the plate, or to first base, he must complete the throw.
3. When throwing to first base, the pitcher must step directly toward the base.
4. The pitcher must not drop the ball in the middle of his delivery.
5. When he wants to chase down a base runner, the pitcher must step back off the rubber.

6. The pitcher must pause for one second in the stretch position before pitching the ball to the plate.
7. When he does not have the ball, the pitcher must make no false appearance to pitch.

Pick-off play

A successful pick-off play requires perfect timing, since the throw is usually made before the shortstop actually gets to the bag. The shortstop generally teams with the pitcher because he plays behind the runner. The play is usually attempted when the run, if scored, might have a final bearing on the game. A good time to work the pick-off play is when the count is three balls and one strike, or three balls and two strikes, because the runner is frequently given the "go" sign in these situations.

Unquestionably, the pick-off play must be practiced over and over until the timing between the pitcher and infielder is synchronized perfectly, so that the throw can be made quickly and accurately.

There are several basic methods of working the pick-off play at second base.

Method 1 The pitcher gives a signal to the shortstop, such as rubbing his shirt with his pitching hand. The shortstop answers with a similar signal. The pitcher takes his pitching position, while looking toward the runner. When the pitcher turns his head toward the plate, the shortstop immediately breaks for the bag. The pitcher looks momentarily toward the batter, then turns and makes his throw.

Method 2 When the shortstop thinks the runner is off guard, he breaks for the bag. The shortstop may break for second base after retreating toward the runner's left. This retreat, in which he backs up slowly, serves as a signal to the pitcher. The runner feels the shortstop has retreated back to his original position, but actually, it keeps him about the same distance from the bag. In either case, the pitcher should watch the shortstop so that he can turn and throw as soon as the break is made for the bag.

Method 3 (The daylight play) The shortstop initiates this play by placing daylight between himself and the runner. The pitcher uses his own judgment. The time to throw is when the pitcher sees daylight between the shortstop and the runner--with the shortstop closer to the bag.

Method 4 (Count play) A signal from the shortstop starts this play When the runner at second takes an extra long lead, he becomes "fair game" for a pick-off play. While the pitcher is looking at the runner, the shortstop flashes the signal. He breaks for the bag as the pitcher turns back to face the batter. As the pitcher turns toward the plate, he counts "ONE-TWO" and turns and throws on "THREE." The shortstop starts on the count of "TWO."

The throw should be knee-high and directly over the bag, in order for the shortstop to make a sure catch and a quick tag.

Fielding his position

The pitcher has the important responsibility of being the "fifth infielder." Many times, the difference between winning and losing rests on the fielding skill of the pitcher. Handling batted balls hit up the middle, fielding bunts, throwing accurately to the right base, covering, and backing up bases are just some of the key responsibilities of the pitcher. The moment the ball leaves his fingertips, the pitcher becomes the "fifth infielder." The pitcher should follow through and be ready for the ball to be hit back at him at all times, and be well balanced, with his feet spread, ready to go either way, the glove in front of the body.

Indeed, a pitcher can help himself by fielding his position efficiently. His ability to handle batted balls and diagnose play situations can be as important to his success on the mound as the manner in which he delivers the baseball to the plate.

Fielding a bunt

On bunt plays, the pitcher must break for the ball as fast as he can. As he nears the ball, he should slow down a little, keeping his eyes on the ball all the time. A right-handed pitcher should try to get in front of the ball. He should jam his right foot hard into the ground, with his body bending at the waist. Using two hands, he picks up the ball. His eyes follow the ball into his glove. Raising up to a throwing position, he turns to his left and throws.

The left-handed pitcher should face the third base line, with his right foot closer than the left to the line, and turn to his right to make the throw.

On a bunt down the first base line, the pitcher should try to get in front of the ball. If it is close to the line, he should make the throw to the inside of first base.

Good judgment by the pitcher is essential in bunts and slow rollers down the foul lines. He must decide whether to field the ball or let it roll, in the hope it will roll foul. As soon as it moves into foul territory, he slaps it with his bare or gloved hand. If the pitcher feels the bunt is on, he should make his first pitch a fast ball just above the strike zone, hoping that it will be popped up. He should wait until the ball is bunted, and then break.

Throwing to first

When fielding a bunt, the pitcher should use two hands whenever possible. His glove acts as the shovel, with his bare hand scooping the ball into it. Both hands should come up together toward his shoulder as the pitcher plants his right foot firmly in the ground. He should pivot, look to first, take a little step and throw to the first baseman. He should have his eyes on the first baseman's chest while making an overhand throw. He should never lob the ball, and always put something on the throw. In fielding the bunt, the pitcher should spin toward his glove hand in throwing to first, second, or third. He should make the safe play early in the game, or when in doubt where to throw.

Throwing to second

On a ball hit back to him, or when fielding a bunt, the pitcher must know who is going to cover second. With a runner on first, he should always ask the second baseman and shortstop who will cover. The catcher directs the action on these fielding plays, and the pitcher must listen to him yell "second" or "first."

On double play balls, the ball should be thrown to the infielder covering the bag, chest-high, leading the shortstop slightly, or to the second baseman, who then makes his pivot.

The pitcher must concentrate on making his throw

accurately. Therefore, he must not hurry his throw or make it while off balance.

Throwing to third

One of the toughest plays for the defense to handle is the bunt or slow hit ball down the third base line. On this big play, the defense should strive to get the lead runner going into third. However, if this is impossible, they must go for the out at first or second base. The pitcher has the responsibility for fielding the ball hit to his third base side, with the third baseman moving back toward the base and receiving the throw.

The key to the play is the third baseman. He must make the decision the moment the ball is hit, as to whether the pitcher can field the ball. If not, he immediately yells, "I got it!" and makes the throw to first or second base. To get the important force play at third base, the pitcher must practice moving off the mound quickly and making an accurate throw to the third baseman.

Covering first base

On any ball hit to his left, the pitcher should automatically break toward first base. Many games have been lost because the pitcher failed to get off the mound in time.

There are two methods of performing this play:

Method 1 On a ball hit to the first baseman's left, or straight to him, the pitcher should circle into the bag. He runs to a spot about twelve to fifteen feet in front of the base and approaches the base running parallel to the line. As he gets near the base, he should slow down slightly and bring his speed under control.

The ball should get to the pitcher a good stride from first base. Catching the ball chest-high, the pitcher now has the opportunity to locate the bag and tag it. He should whirl around over his left shoulder, ready to make a play on any other runner.

Method 2 On a ball hit to the right of the first baseman, or on a slow roller, the pitcher should go directly to the bag and anchor there. This also applies to the first-second-first double play with the shortstop.

On a fumble, the pitcher should stop, place one foot on the second base side of the bag and be ready to stretch or shift to either side for the throw

On slow hit balls to his first base side, if the pitcher can field the ball himself, he should yell out: "I've got it." Then, the first baseman should answer: "Take it" The first baseman will then cover the base. While this seems quite simple, it is very important.

Covering home

When there is a man on third base and a passed ball or wild pitch occurs, the pitcher must be alert to cover the plate. In fact, anytime the catcher is drawn away from the home plate area, the pitcher must be ready to cover. Coming in as fast as he can, the pitcher should drop down on his knee, facing the intended throw. He should give the runner the outside half of the plate. Straddling the inside half of the plate, he gives the runner the outside or foul line territory. He does not want to block the plate, because of the possibility of getting cut up. He tags the runner with the back of his glove facing him.

Backing up bases

Every ball that goes to the outfield is a potential backup play for the pitcher, regardless of the number of runners on base. Once he has decided to which base the throw is likely to be made, the pitcher runs to a point forty to fifty feet behind that base, and in line with the player who is making the throw. From this position on the diamond, he can easily retrieve all balls which may rebound past the intended receiver. If he is in doubt as to which base to back up, the pitcher should take a position between bases until the outfielder makes his throw. He should always be one base ahead of the lead runner.

Pitch-out

A pitch-out is a deliberate waste ball that the batter cannot possibly reach. The purpose of this pitch is to permit the catcher to throw to one of the bases, for runners who take long leads. Or, it might be used when an attempted steal, hit and run, or squeeze play is anticipated. The pitcher usually throws a shoulder-high fast ball on a pitch-out sign. He tries to keep the ball high and far outside the plate. A pitch-out is released more quickly, using a snap overhand throw.

One of the cardinal rules of baseball is, "Never walk the tying or winning run intentionally." While there are situations when walking a hitter intentionally can be justified, the percentages are heavily in favor of the defense.

Intentional pass

In giving an intentional pass, the pitcher should not lob the ball to the plate, but throw medium-speed fast balls about three feet outside and shoulder-high.

Since he cannot leave the catcher's area until the pitcher releases the ball, the catcher makes his target by holding the glove far out to the side and then takes a lateral step to receive the ball. The primary objective of the intentional pass is to pitch to a more logical opponent, while setting up a force or possible double play. It is used only with first base open.

Another time the intentional pass is considered good baseball is with the winning run on third, and either none or only one of the other bases occupied.

Moving a hitter back

The inside-outside style of pitching is a regular practice of major league pitchers, particularly for hitters who crowd the plate. This means that a pitcher should learn to throw his fast ball on the inside in order to keep the hitter from covering up the outside of the plate. Pitchers who throw too much on the outside, without an occasional inside pitch, will soon have the hitters taking picks on the seemingly "perfect pitches" that hit the low outside corner. By keeping all his pitches out over the plate, a pitcher is simply inviting the hitters to take a toehold and swing from the heels.

Pitching inside refers to the practice of throwing hard stuff in and off the plate from four to twelve inches. "We make a major effort to 'jam' the hitter, make him hit the ball near his hands," explained Cluck. "By pitching inside regularly, we make our other pitches more effective. Hitting is 'timing' and nothing destroys a hitter's timing faster than to be 'jammed'."

Larry Sherry, who was a fine relief pitcher with us early in the 1960s, had a theory on handling the batter who constantly crowded the plate. "Anyone who moves into the plate or stands close to the plate," said Larry, "you have to pitch tight.

Occasionally, a pitcher may come in too tight and knock down a hitter. This gives the impression that he is throwing a duster, but more than likely, his fast ball just took off. Drysdale was blamed for many pitches inside that he did not intentionally throw because his fast ball was a live one that would bear in and down. Koufax, on the other hand, seldom brushed anybody back. A good time to brush a hitter back is with two strikes and no balls. However, a pitcher should never throw at the hitter with the intention of hitting him.

Warming up

A pitcher should always warm up, get good and loose and break a little sweat, before he starts to throw hard or run hard, in order not to strain or pull any muscles. Fifteen minutes of warm-up should be enough for any starting pitcher. The opening minutes should be devoted to loosening up from both the windup and stretch positions. The last seven minutes should get the pitcher good and loose, ready to face the first hitter.

Relief pitchers sometimes have to enter a ball game with only a few minutes of warm-up.

The following are tips on warming up:

1. Always throw at a target.
2. Throw easy at first, but with your whole delivery.
3. Use straight stuff at first.
4. Start throwing breaking pitches by just twisting or spinning the ball.

5. Practice working from the set position.
6. Move the ball around--up and down, in and out.
7. Spend more time on the pitch that is not working right.
8. Make sure you are good and loose before you start throwing hard.

Working on the hitter

The ability to work on the hitter plays an increasingly vital role as the pitcher advances upward in baseball. A pitcher can have all the stuff in the world, but without control, a variety of pitches, and the ability to set up the hitter, his live fast ball and sharp curve can be greatly reduced in effectiveness. As he progresses in baseball, a pitcher should learn how to go to work on the hitter, trying to make him hit his best pitch.

The secret of good hitting is timing, so the batter must be kept off balance. A pitcher can disrupt the hitter's timing by throwing the ball at different speeds with the same motion. The hitter who is kept off balance never seems to get his pitch. The key to containing good hitters is to get ahead of them and not give them anything good. Fernando Valenzuela relies on mixing up his pitches, changing speeds, and nipping the corners. He gets hitters looking for one thing, then gives them something else.

A number of factors affect a pitching pattern, including the score, inning, outs, runners on base, type of hitter, and the pitcher himself. As a result, the pattern and sequence of pitches should vary from pitch to pitch.

An experienced pitcher will take advantage of the weaknesses of the hitters, and his pitching pattern will be arranged accordingly. It is important that every pitch have an element of surprise.

By establishing a pattern, the pitcher can set up the hitter for his "out pitch," one which the batter is weakest at hitting. Having been set up, the hitter is made more vulnerable. Southpaw Jerry Reuss, for example, is very effective throwing his hard stuff in on the right-handed hitters. We used to tell pitchers to crowd them with hard stuff. Those big guys like to extend their arms. Pitchers like Valenzuela and Tug McGraw, who have a specialty, work in this fashion. To be effective, they rely on their "off pitches," such as screwballs and sinker pitches. By setting him up, they make the hitter hit their best pitch.

Valenzuela has five pitches in his repertoire, and rarely does the hitter see the same pitch twice. This is because he mixes his pitches, changing speeds and moving the ball around. In addition to his famous screwball, Valenzuela can effectively throw the curve, slider, and change-up, but his fast ball sets up the rest of his pitches. If you can't back up the screwball with a fast one, the smart hitter just waits.

Even the top pitcher does not always have the good fast ball every time he pitches. This is when he has to be a pitcher, and not a thrower. The thrower tries to force his fast ball, even when he does not have it. Instead, he should go to his breaking stuff and begin changing speeds and hitting the corners.

A pitcher should not try to strike everyone out. He will just tire himself out, and will press and often force his pitching. He should use his players. They will know he can get the ball over the plate, and in turn, they will come up with better plays. By conserving his energy and the number of pitches, he can call for a little more reserve energy when he gets into tough situations in the later innings.

Get ahead of the hitter

The pitcher should get his first pitch over the plate with something on it If he can stay ahead of the hitter, a pitcher's troubles will be greatly reduced. He should try to get ahead of the batter and force him to hit his pitch. With two strikes on the hitter, a pitcher should want the hitter to go for his best pitch.

If he is ahead of the hitter, he might push him back once or twice before going for the decisive pitch. On a one-ball-and-two-strike count, Steve Carlton's fourth pitch is high and tight, which moves the hitter back from the plate. He follows with a hard slider to the outside corner. In a crucial situation, the pitcher will either go to the hitter's weakness for a double play, or he may go to his own strength and strike him out

The following should be observed when working on the hitter:

1. Get the ball over the plate with good stuff on it.
2. With men on base, keep your pitches down.
3. Try to get ahead of the hitter. Then, go to work!
4. Move the ball around, in and out, up and down, keeping the batter off balance.
5. Change the speeds of the pitches.

6. Learn the batter's strengths and weaknesses.
7. Observe the hitter's position, stance, and stride.
8. Work on the corners when ahead of the hitter.
9. A waste pitch should be off the plate but close enough to tempt the hitter.
10. Do not throw the same pitch in the same area too often.
11. Do not show everything. Save your strength pitches for key situations.
12. Do not be reluctant to pit your strength against the batter's strength
13. Have a reason for throwing each pitch. "Why am I throwing this pitch?"
14. Brush back the hitter who crowds the plate.
15. Do not work too slowly or too fast.
16. After two strikes, make the batter hit your pitch.
17. Use your best controlled pitch to get ahead and stick to what you do best.
18. As the old adage goes, "When in doubt--curve him." This is because most ball players are fast ball hitters.
19. Let your fielders do their work.

Types of hitters

Type	*suggestion*
1. Open stance hitter	Since he likes inside pitches, keep them away from him.
2. Long stride hitter	Usually a low ball hitter--pitch him high

3. Uppercut hitter	Pitch him high and tight
4. Crouch hitter	Since he likes low pitching, pitch him high.
5. Lunge hitter	Use a change-up or a high, tight fast ball.
6. Hitch hitter	Pitch him fast and tight, although changing up is often effective.
7. Nervous, overanxious hitter	Take your time and make him wait.
8. Bucket hitter	Give him outside pitches, particularly curves.
9. Hitter who turns his head	Give him some curves, particularly on the outside pitch
10. "Guess" hitter	Mix up your pitches.

Relief pitching

A good relief pitcher is one who can come in out of the bullpen, without taking too much time to get ready, and be able to throw strikes. He cannot afford to get behind the hitter. He must get ahead of him quickly.

A good bullpen has become the backbone of a major league pitching staff. It is also a big plus for high school and college teams to have a pitcher who can come in and stop the opposition late in the game. Don McMahon, pitching coach of the Cleveland Indians, pointed out: "Whether or not school teams have designated specialists, we do feel the coach should give everyone on his staff a thorough understanding of relief pitching, such as warming up effectively, training physically and mentally, and what to do when entering a tight game."

The heavy work given today's relief pitchers suggests that a pitcher is capable of pitching more often than was previously thought possible. Normally, relief pitchers who throw extremely hard and pitch two or three innings one day can come back for an inning the next day. Dave Guisti, former relief pitcher of the Pittsburg Pirates, explained: "if I went two innings, I could come back for two innings the next day, perhaps even three days in a row, and then have to take a day off. But throwing too often can take something out of you."

"Temperament is a key factor in the success of a relief pitcher," stated Ron Perranoski, pitching coach of the Dodgers and a former top relief pitcher. "You just cannot get excited out there. Even though one mistake can cost your team the ball game, you cannot let this bother you. You just have to feel that there will be another game tomorrow."

Baseball's most effective relievers have the ability to make the ball sink or keep it down for a possible double play. Ideally, a good relief man should have keep it down for a possible at least two pitches that he can throw for a strike anytime he wants to. If he can control his third pitch, he will make a good stopper in anybody's league.

Before a ball game

Big-league relief pitchers do their conditioning during pregame practice. They arrive on the field early and shag for the hitters, in addition to taking some cuts themselves. Generally, relief men do about eight wind sprints daily, compared to about twelve to fifteen for starting pitchers. McMahon likes the relief pitcher's routine of pitching some before the game. "I always liked to throw three-quarters or half-speed, perhaps five or six minutes on the side, just to find out if I had my rhythm and my arm was loose. In the late innings, you might have to get up quickly and not have your full time to loosen up."

Getting ready

Relief pitching has become such a specialized phase of the game that each major league team has a short man, as well as middle and long relievers. "I know my position is going to be as the short man," said Perranoski, "from the seventh inning on. Therefore, from about the fourth inning, we prepare myself mentally, sitting in the bullpen and watching the ball game. We have to know what pitcher is on the mound and how long my manager will go with him. I must know who the hitter is, and who the next two hitters will be. We have to know how many runs we are ahead or behind."

As far as preparing himself physically to get loosened up, with Perranoski, it varies from day to day. "If we have pitched on four or five straight days," said Ron, "it may take me a little longer to get loose because of stiffness. But if we have had two or three days of rest, we can get ready sometimes after ten to twelve pitches, plus the eight on the mound. There are, of course, so many variables, such as the weather condition. If it is cold, naturally, it will take longer."

In warming up, the relief pitcher should begin his throwing with easy, slow speed pitches. He should not warm up with full velocity right away. When you have to get ready in a hurry, the easiest way to do it is to throw off-speed breaking pitches and really overexaggerate the follow-through.

Coming in from the bullpen

The relief pitcher has to know the situation: how many men are on, the score, and who are the hitters. "Usually, if a left-handed hitter is coming up to the plate," asserted Perranoski, "I can expect they will switch to a right-handed pinch hitter. "The first pitch is the most important pitch in a tough situation. It is not a matter of just throwing the ball over for a strike. Rather, it is a matter of hitting a particular spot."

"I want my relievers to come in and throw strikes," said Johnny McNamara, manager of the California Angels. "I also want them to get some hum on the ball."

Getting the job done

"I try to concentrate on throwing a sinking fast ball," explained Perranoski. "I have to keep the ball down because I am not an overpowering pitcher. We will throw an occasional curve, even taking some speed off of it, which makes my fast ball look a little faster.

Conditioning of the pitcher

Some pitchers have the mistaken idea that in order to get into condition, all they have to do is throw, and throw, and get their arms in shape. As a result, after five or six innings, when their legs give out, they rest under a warm shower.

Pitchers should always keep in mind that "a pitcher's legs are just as important as his arm." The entire body must be in good physical condition in order to prevent sore arms. Whenever a pitcher does not bend the knees of his pivot foot, he is either a lazy pitcher or a poorly conditioned one. He must have spring in his legs. During the season, pitchers must follow a regular schedule in order to get the necessary throwing and running between starts. Therefore, we want our pitchers to run a lot. Running is the most important way to exercise. Even after the season begins, we want our pitchers to run twenty to twenty-five minutes daily when they are not scheduled to work.

Besides their daily running, most pitchers keep in condition through pepper practice, pickups, and shagging balls. Football pass drills, fungo drills, and fielding drills will provide needed variety. Getting pitchers in shape for the coming season is certainly simpler when they have had a good winter program. Then, some coaches feel the best way to be a pitcher is to throw the ball properly and often.

Strength development

Many pitchers can attribute their success in part to well planned weight-resistance programs during the off-season. These programs of strength development involve use of weights, apparatus, calisthenics, or isometric training. All of these items could be included in a sound program, which must be closely supervised by coaches.

Stretching is the key to the entire weight training program for pitchers. Without stretching, the program could prove damaging. The pitcher must stretch after each exercise period to maintain flexibility. Never allow a pitcher to lift weights without stretching afterward. In any strength-building program, it is important to continually increase the amount of resistance. The muscles being developed have to be overloaded, starting first with few repetitions, and bringing more muscle fibers into play to overcome the resistance. The result is growth in strength. However, caution should be taken to limit the weight lifted.

Calisthenics alone lack the efficiency of weights and apparatus as a strength developer. It just takes too long to overload a muscle group through calisthenics. However, they do have considerable value in maintaining body flexibility and as a warm-up activity.

Care of the arm

If he is scheduled to pitch the next day, a big league pitcher generally comes in before the previous day's game and gets a massage and stretching, which lasts about twenty minutes. On the day of a game, a half-hour before starting his warm-up, he comes in for a massage and a light stretch. Most big-league trainers use Capsolin for this purpose because, when the body perspires, the perspiration comes through the Capsolin. Analgesic, atomic bomb, and Logangesic seem to hold the perspiration to the body. Sometimes trainers mix the Capsolin with baby oil. On the day after a game, a pitcher will likely jog around, throw, and play a little pepper. The next day, two days before his pitching turn, he will go out and play "long toss" in the outfield. He will throw 120 or 150 feet, just to stretch out his arm, not worrying about velocity.

Ice bag technique

After the game is over, all of our pitchers use the ice

bag technique made famous by Sandy Koufax and Drysdale. Today, most teams have their pitchers use immersion, soaking the arm in ice for about a half-hour. In the case of Drysdale, his arm was elevated and ice bags were used all the way from his wrist to his mid-back for about twenty-five minutes. Then he was given a very light stretch, which helped him with his elbow problem and got him ready about one day sooner.

Jogging, though, is better for the off-season. An athlete has to jog so much farther and longer to do the same thing he can do with his sprints.

To avoid arm trouble, advice to the young pitcher is:

1. Build up a strong arm and body through regular throwing, running, and exercise.
2. Concentrate on the fast ball until you have built up a strong, flexible arm.
3. Forget about the breaking pitches, especially the slider, until you have matured physically.
4. Never throw hard until you are completely warmed up.
5. Do not pitch too often in competition. Make sure you have the proper amount of rest between starts.
6. Regular throwing is not only the greatest deterrent to a sore arm, but, often the best remedy for it.

Pitching in a rotation system

Major league starting pitchers follow either a four-day or five-day pitching plan. The pitcher's arm, the schedule, and the strength of the staff are the determining factors in the rotation plan. During the last half of the season, I think the five-day rotation is better, but early in the season, with more rain outs and more days off, a team can get by with a three or four man pitching rotation. As the season progresses, with more doubleheaders and fewer off days, it is better to go with a pitching staff of five.

To a large extent, all this depends on the individuals who make up the staff. Some pitchers work better with four days' rest. The size of the staff is a factor too. A team may have only two or three effective starting pitchers. Seaver, for example, pitches every fifth day. If he starts on Sunday, he rests on Monday. Then he throws for about fifteen or twenty minutes on Tuesday, and rests again on Wednesday and Thursday before he pitches on Friday.

Typical pitching schedule

A typical major league pitching schedule is as follows (five-day plan):

Sunday: Pitch a nine-inning game.

Monday: Rest (do not touch a ball, but run in the outfield).

Tuesday: Loosen up (fifteen minutes of light throwing to the catcher).

Wednesday: A good workout (after loosening up, pitch batting practice).

Thursday: No throwing, but good leg work.

Friday: Pitch a nine-inning game.

Clothing and equipment

The shirt should be loose, not binding. Pitchers like the

arm sleeves to be cut just below the elbow. They should be 50/50 cotton and wool or 100 percent wool in the arms. Professional pitchers have fouror five of each. Most pitchers like their toe plate built into their shoe. They should always have a protective plastic cup inside the supporter.

Drills

Drills must be engaged in vigorously, whether they involve covering first base, fielding bunts, throwing to the bases, throwing for the double play, or backing up throws. A pitcher must adapt himself mentally in these drills. The biggest mistake he can make is to just go through the motions. If he performs these skills correctly in practice, very likely they will carry over and become automatic in the game. This is why he must bounce off the mound and hustle after the ball and make this play correctly in practice. Pitchers who appear bored and handle their assignments sloppily during practice invariably are the ones who foul up in game situations--and one miscue can lose the ball game for him and his team.

Covering first base

The pitchers should line up near the mound, one behind the other, each with a ball. The coach is at home plate with a ball and fungo bat, and the catcher positions himself behind the plate.

The pitcher throws to the catcher, and the coach hits the ball toward first base. The pitcher then runs to cover first, taking the throw from the first baseman. Then the pitcher goes to the end of the line, and the process continues as the catcher gives the coach the ball he caught from the previous pitcher.

The coach can keep the pitcher from cheating by hitting an occasional grounder through the box.

Throwing to first base

This drill not only provides the pitcher valuable lessons in keeping the runner close to first base, but it serves other purposes as well. The base runner gets experience in taking a good lead, and the defense can work on their responsibilities. The pitchers form a line behind the mound, while the base runners form a line at the first base coaching box. The pitcher tries to prevent the runner from taking too big a lead, and he may throw over to the first baseman, attempting to pick off the runner.

This drill gives the pitcher practice in making the delivery to home plate from his set position. The coach watches the pitcher closely to detect any balk motion.

Backing up bases

A good drill for backing up bases is to put the pitcher on the mound and have him go through various game conditions with runners on base. This is the same procedure used in cutoff play practice. The pitcher also covers a base that is unguarded because the catcher or an infielder has left his position.

Pick-off play

This drill gives the pitcher practice in pivoting and picking runners off second base. The pitchers form a line off to the first base side of the mound, while one of them takes his set position on the rubber. The runner assumes his lead off second base. The second baseman and shortstop get in their playing positions and work a pick-off play with the pitcher.

The base runner can allow the pick-off to succeed at first, since the defensive players need practice in executing this play.

Throw-catch

The pitchers line up at the foul line in right field, facing center field. Each pitcher has his glove and a ball. A coach or reserve player stands halfway to center field. The first pitcher runs toward the coach. When he is ten or fifteen yards away, he throws him the ball. After catching it, the coach permits the pitcher to run past and then returns the ball to the pitcher by giving him a lead throw.

Pepper

One or more players throws the ball to a hitter, who hits grounders and liners to the fielders, who are about fifteen feet away. This drill has more value when the fielders are limited to just two or three individuals. A game can be made of this fine drill, with the fielders counting how many consecutive times they can catch a ball without error.

Pickups

The purpose of this drill is to get the pitcher to move quickly from side to side and to pick up slow rolling balls. The pitchers pair off about twelve feet apart, one acting as the tosser and the other as the fielder. The tosser rolls the ball first to one side and then to the other side of the pitcher.

Upon fielding the ball, it is returned to the tosser and the fielder keeps fielding the ball until he has fielded fifty of them. Then, they change places.

3

CATCHING

The catcher has to be the leader, a take-charge sort of person who can direct the play of his team. His performance behind the plate, in handling his pitchers, keeping the runners honest with a strong and accurate arm, setting up the hitters, and keeping the whole team inspired and alert by being aggressive and full of drive, contributes to the effectiveness of the pitcher out on the mound. Since they are all watching him, the catcher can set a good example for the defensive team.

Indeed, a team's greatest need is a skilled, clever, and spirited catcher. I do not think a team can rise to championship heights without an able and durable receiver. The confidence of not only the pitcher, but the entire defense, rests on the catcher. He must know the weakness of opposing hitters, be able to handle all types of pitches and Fielding plays, and be able to throw with strength and accuracy.

The essentials

A strong arm can be a great asset to the catcher and his team. In fact, a player cannot hope to be a successful catcher if he does not have a strong throwing arm. He must be able to throw base runners out with consistency and keep opponents from stealing and taking extra bases.

On some occasions, the catcher may have to go out to the mound and give his pitcher some encouragement and suggestions. "Don't try to throw too hard," or, "Don't rush your motion" are typical of the little reminders the catcher can give the pitcher. A receiver often has to remind his pitcher to throw to first base and be alert for a bunt play. If the ball is hit back to him, where will he throw the ball? How many outs, and what is the score? This is why the catcher has to be a good leader and a quarterback on the ball field.

Catching the low ball and throwing to the bases are two of the most important skills of a good catcher. Therefore, the receiver should practice catching the low ball as much as he can, and work diligently on his throwing. Correct footwork in shifting for the throw is essential. Catching is a vigorous activity and demands considerable endurance. Stopping a low pitch with the body and getting a foul tip on the "meat hand" goes with the job. Perhaps this is why the catching job calls for more dedication than any other position in the game. He has to *want* to catch!

Qualifications

A catcher has to be able to catch the ball. While this basic skill sounds elementary, the ability of the receiver to handle all types of pitched and thrown balls, bunts, and pop fouls can be a major factor in a "sound defense."

Being able to catch low throws, particularly, is of great importance in instilling the confider ce of the pitcher in keeping his pitches down. Quite often, a pitcher is reluctant to throw a low curve ball with a man on third base, fearful that it might bounce in the dirt and get past the catcher.

Talking to and encouraging the pitcher can help make the pitcher think he can get the hitter out. Jeff Torborg had that encouragement quality. He would go out to the mound and say, "Come on, Bill, let's get this guy!" When he made a good pitch, Jeff would say, "That was a great pitch!" A catcher has to be kind of a cheerleader. His confidence actually will reflect on the pitcher. To me, this is one of the most important attributes of an outstanding receiver.

A catcher must learn to understand each and every pitcher as a different individual. He must converse with his pitchers at all times to develop good rapport, a relationship necessary for a smooth-working battery.

Another requirement is the ability to block the plate—a rugged, rough catcher who is not afraid of a little body contact. Those runners come in there with a full force, and he has to block the plate, catch the ball and tag the runner, all at the same time. Therefore, the catcher has to be a rugged individual, with a lot of courage.

A good receiver has to have fair size in order to take all the abuse that he will have to take. Yet, mobility, the ability to bounce around, fielding bunts, shifting on bad pitches, and getting foul balls, is even more important.'

Type of glove

The single or double break glove is the dominant type used today. The "one-handed glove" has a break like a first baseman's glove. Until the mid-seventies, there were two types of gloves worn by catchers: 1) the single-break glove and 2) the non-hinged glove. The major baseball glove companies, however, are no longer manufacturing the non-hinged glove.

Single-break globe

All major league receivers use a glove with one or two breaks in it. The one-handed glove is very similar to the type used by the first baseman. Johnny Bench, for many years the game's top receiver, explained that "with a one-handed glove, I can keep my meat hand away from or behind the glove, and I seem to have more manoeuvrability with a single-break mitt."

Rawlings Company has their Johnny Bench Professional models featuring a crotch-laced, high pocket web with a spiral-laced top, a single-break heel which offers an adjustable thumb and little finger loops. Wilson Company has a Professional Twin Action mitt made of premium cowhide leather, a double-break mitt with a Pro-Back design. It features the "Pro Toe" and dual-horizontal-hinge web.

The new types of single or double break gloves are very much like a first base glove. I believe the one-handed receiver behind the plate can do a fine job unless he becomes lazy and forms bad habits about shifting on pitches.

Non-handed catching

This traditional type of glove, until it was replaced by the single-break model, forced the receiver to become a better "two-handed catcher." A non-hinged mitt forced the catcher to catch with two hands and execute proper footwork. He had to shift to his right and left. The non-hinged glove helped the catcher learn the rhythmic footwork and obtain the proper balance necessary for accurate throwing.

One-handed catching

One-handed catching evolved primarily to protect the throwing hand from foul balls. The improved make of the catcher's glove has made one-handed receiving more convenient. Since they facilitate one-handed catching, the single or double break gloves are now highly popular among catchers.

One-handed receiving is particularly the rule today with no runners on base. Many catchers will even put their throwing hand behind them for added protection. One-handed receivers, however, catch almost every pitch near the webbing deep into the glove, and they often have difficulty getting a hold of the ball and moving it into throwing position. With runners on base, rather than use the webbing, one-handed catchers should try to catch the ball closer to the center of the pocket and the palm where control and feel is better. To reduce the pain of catching pitches in the palm, many catchers will have additional padding in the palm or wear a golf or handball glove.

With runners on base, the one-handed catcher should not position his throwing hand too far away from the mitt. Even the catcher using a hinged glove can use the two-handed technique by placing his bare hand on or near the glove for quicker exchange.

With no runners on, catcher Gary Carter rests his right hand behind his leg. With a runner on first base, however, he has his hand by the glove.

There is no doubt that the two-handed catcher is better than the one-handed catcher. He shifts better, blocks pitches better, and throws more quickly. However, catching the ball behind the plate with two hands is certainly more dangerous in that there is a greater possibility of a broken finger on the throwing hand. This is the major reason for catching one-handed, which is not a bad reason since the loss of the catcher for several weeks can hurt a team badly.

Target

The catcher should give the pitcher a good target. Above all, he should give him a full target. After giving the signal from his crouch, he moves slowly into his ready stance, with the glove in the middle of his body. He should keep the target arm away from his body, flexed, and with encouraging gestures. He also gives his target at the spot where he wants the pitch.

To give an outside target, the catcher merely has to move about six inches farther than the normal target over the middle. When he wants to give a target on the inside, he merely has to move over six inches to his left. Many pitchers prefer this type to that of merely extending the glove into the area desired.

"If I want the ball slightly on the inside corner," said Del Crandall, one of baseball's former great catchers with the Milwaukee Braves, "I will move over prior to giving my signal. If you remain in the middle of the plate to give the signal and then move your body and glove over, you will likely tip off the hitter. "Furthermore, if the catcher can keep his body in front of the pitch, plus his target, the pitchers seem to have better control."

Holding the hand

There are several ways that catchers hold their bare hands. Some receivers like to "cup their hand," with the fingers bent a little and the thumb touching the index finger. Another method is to close the fingers loosely, with the index finger folded over the thumb. However, the hand should not be clenched tightly. The important point in holding the hand is that the fingers are not pointed toward the pitcher, but are curled. "I try to keep the hand loose," said Johnny Bench, "sort of a relaxed fist, like you are holding a piece of cotton, with your thumb inside your fingers to keep them from getting damaged. Should the ball 4 hit them, you will have some cushion on your fingers so that they will give." A catcher is asking for trouble when he holds the meat hand up to the side and away from the glove hand.

Giving signals

There are many different methods of giving signs. Generally, our receivers use a combination of signals. They might give the location with the flaps, and then give the pitch with the fingers. With nobody on base, most catchers use the single series; that is, one finger for the fast ball, two fingers for the curve ball, and a wiggling of the fingers for the change-of-pace. For the slow curve, two fingers are slowly flexed and extended. Some teams use a fist for a pitchout.

If there is a runner on second base, the catcher should use a sign series which is more difficult to understand, so that the runner cannot relay the pitches to the hitter. One method is to give a series of three signs, with the first, second, or third the actual sign. Another method is to add the first and third signs. If they total two, it is a fast ball; three, a curve; four, a change; five, a pitchout. Many big-league catchers use a hand sign to indicate whether they want the ball to be high, low, inside, or outside. These are called *location signs.* If our receivers want the ball high and inside, they give one sign for that location and then the type of pitch it is. However, the catcher should not get his glove up to the desired target too soon, so that everybody in the ball park knows where that pitch is coming. The catcher should signal first the *type* of pitch, then give the *direction* of the pitch. Sometimes, however, catchers will signal the location first, and then the pitch.

Before the game, as well as between innings, the catcher should go over the hitters with the manager and pitchers. Hand signals are often used for night ball and whenever the pitcher has trouble seeing them because of shadows. The catcher can "flick" his fingers out a certain number of times for the various pitches. Whatever signs are used, they should be kept relatively simple and yet not easy enough for the opposition to pick up.

Signals can also be given by the c off base. Signs that can be used are wiping a hand across the chest protector, grabbing the face mask, or throwing dirt off to the side. The infielder should give an answer back that the play is on, so the ball is not thrown away. After the pick-off sign is flashed and answered, the receiver then gives a pitchout sign to the pitcher. Fielders should not leave their position unless the pitchout is given.

Switching signals

To switch a signal, a son is given that alters the meaning of the signs in the series. This prevents the opposing team from picking up the signal pattern, particularly with a man on second. The catcher may hold the right hand on the knee with the fingers together to shift the sign from the second to the third showing of the fingers. The pitcher should indicate to the catcher that fie has observed the switch by returning a prearranged signal, possibly by touching the peak of his cap. Still further, the battery can use the switch signal to change from a curve to a fast ball.

Stance

Catchers have two sets of stances: 1) a signal-giving stance and 2) a ready stance, the receiving position. Regardless of the type of stance, it must be comfortable, since catching is a very tiring job. The more comfortable the catcher can be, the better off he is. Since every catcher has a different physical build, what will work for him might not be best for another receiver.

Signal position

In giving signs, the catcher must assume a stance in which he can hide all his signals and prevent his opponents from stealing them. This is not the same stance he catches from. He merely gives his signs from this position. Hanging his glove over his left knee, he gives the signs over his right leg, deep in the crotch. The left forearm rests on the thigh, with the mitt hand in front of and next to the left knee, with the front of the glove facing in toward the crotch.

"The right leg must go straight to the pitcher," explained Torborg, "and that blocks out all the signs from the first base coach. To block out signs from the third base coach, the glove hand, the left hand, should be held little past the knee of the left leg. Some catchers sit a little higher than others, but they should be sitting down easily."

"When you start to give the signs," continued Jeff, "you have to keep your right arm in tight toward your body. You don't want the elbow sticking out away from the body because, if you do, your arm will move and increase the chance of giving away the signal. Therefore, you clamp it down tight."

Receiving position

After he comes out of the sign-giving stance, the catcher gets up into the ready position to receive the ball. To be able to throw or field a bunt, he must have a stance which is not only comfortable but which he feels, he can get out of quickly Normally, the feet are more than shoulder-width apart The toe of the right foot is about on a line with the heel of the left foot, and pointing toward first base. "In this position, your thighs and lower part of the legs form almost a right angle," explained Torborg. "Your weight is slightly forward on the balls of your feet, however, you don't lift the heels. You are up on the toe of the right foot, and the left foot is planted a little more solidly than the right one."

The catcher should move up under the hitter, but not so close that he interferes with his swing. There are a number of advantages in staying as close to the plate as possible. Among them, he will be in a better position to throw on steals, to move out quickly on bunts, and to handle low pitches easily. He must have a feeling of readiness, to be ready to go. He has to get his weight planted so that he has pretty good weight on his right foot, with a certain amount on the ball of his left foot. He is balanced, ready to move in any direction.

When he crouches down ready for the pitch, the catcher should strive for the most comfortable position he can obtain. Too low a buttocks will definitely restrict his lateral motions. Conversely, if his tail is too high, he will have difficulty looking up and getting his arms up on high pitches. Consequently, he must find the happy medium, assuming a position about knee-high. This will provide the mobility necessary in moving to his right or to his left. The hands and arms are relaxed, and the upper arms and forearms form almost right angles. The arms and elbows should be kept outside his knees, never between them. The mitt is held in the lower area of the strike zone, moving when necessary to either corner of the plate,

In giving a target and getting ready to receive the pitch, the catcher must make sure that his hand is relaxed and not locked. Torborg explained that, "The wrist can be locked if the face of the glove is held too perpendicular to the pitcher. A locked wrist may cause trouble turning the glove to catch a low pitch."

While the buttocks should be up, a catcher's rear end should not be too high. According to the old theory, the catcher should keep his tail up so he can move better. The first thing that happens when he puts his tail up high is that his shoulders go forward, and then it becomes a real strain to look up at his pitcher. Furthermore, on any ball that is high over his head, he will have difficulty in getting his arm up to it.

Receiving

The catcher who can come up with all types of pitches, rising fast balls as well as low curves and sinkers in the dirt, will give the pitcher much needed confidence.

The catcher's hands should be held out away from his body in a relaxed manner. He should handle pitches above the waist with the fingers pointing up and those below the waist with the fingers pointing down. The belt-high pitch can be handled from either above or below. However, he has to be relaxed with the hands! If he keeps rigid, he will go down with the heel of his glove on low pitches.

In receiving the pitch, the catcher should give slightly with his mitt as the ball hits it, at the same time drawing the ball toward his belt buckle. If done smoothly, this will prevent borderline pitches from being moved out of the strike zone. Sloppy catching of pitches may lose a pitcher the strike he deserves. Caution should be taken by the receiver not to block the umpire's view of the ball by excessive jumping movements or body-raising. Too much movement laterally, or up and down, will often take strikes away from the pitcher. A good receiver is smooth and fluid, making as few motions as possible.

On the high pitch, the receiver must remember to get his body in position so that he can field the high ball where he is not cramped. He must get his head and shoulders up, and his tail down. Otherwise, the ball is a pretty easy pitch to miss.

"The problem is the low curve ball," stated Torborg. "First of all, it has a difficult spin on it and does not act normally. It does not bounce directly at you. It usually bounces off to the right or to the left, depending on the spin when it hits the ground."

A big shortcoming of the average receiver is not being alert on every pitch so that, when the runner goes, he is ready to throw. On too many occasions, when the base runner attempts a steal unexpectedly, the catcher is not alert and ready. The catcher has to get into the habit of being ready to throw on every pitch.

Catching more foul tips

Some catchers catch more foul tips than others mainly because they catch up close behind the hitter. In fact, the really good catchers catch as close as possible right behind the hitter. This way, foul tips do not have a chance to veer off that bat as quickly as they would if he were further back. Many young catchers catch too far back, and that is why the ball always gets away from them. Of course, there is a danger zone too. A catcher can be too close. However, if he can be up there where his arms are outstretched, where he can keep them from getting in the way of the bat, he will be a good catcher.

On third strike situations, when there are foul tips off the bat, the ball that is tipped downward has a good chance of being caught. Therefore, a foul-tipped ball is more easily retained when caught with the back of the glove facing the ground.

Handling the low pitch

One of the most crucial plays a catcher has to perform is handling the low pitch. Many a ball game has been decided by a receiver's ability, or lack of it, in stopping the low one in the dirt. The receiver who can handle the low pitches will win the confidence of his pitchers.

For years, baseball coaches have been telling their catchers to "block anything in the dirt." As a result, the accepted practice among most catchers today on the ball in the dirt is to automatically drop their knees first. This is particularly true in some crucial situations. With a man on third base, naturally, the defense does not want to give up a run, so the catcher is instructed to try to block the pitch any way he can. The chief concern is to block the ball and keep it in front of him. Therefore, the catcher is taught to fall to the ground on both knees, with the glove in the middle. By getting the shin guards out of the way, he leaves the soft part of his body for the ball to hit. He keeps his body facing the ball.

Major league catchers like to catch the ball first, and then follow it up with a block. After the receiver moves his hand for the ball, his body comes in with a blocking motion.

This new approach in handling the low pitch can perhaps be attributed to the number of speed merchants on the base, paths. In the past, when catchers tended to block the ball, a fast runner on first would take a base, whether the ball was blocked or not.

Now, many receivers, rather than automatically dropping to their knees, try to catch the ball cleanly, but their body is still in a blocking position should they miss.

The catcher must keep his body square to the pitcher. If the body is on an angle—say, to the right—and the ball hits him, it will still go toward the right. "The important thing here is to keep your mask and chin right in tight to the body," said Torborg, "and looking at the ball all the way. The shoulders and body are square so that if it does hit you, generally, it will bounce out in front of you.

Throwing

For most throws, good body balance is essential for accuracy.. Accuracy and quickness of the throw depends largely on how quickly the catcher can achieve proper balance of his body, along with speed at releasing the ball. The catcher should use the overhand delivery. The only exception is when he fields a bunt or a slow roller while off balance, and must throw sidearm to first or third base. He always uses the overhand throw to second base.

In throwing from the catching position, two important points should always be kept in mind:

1. Try to get the ball off the best way you can.
2. Have a good grip on the ball.

The catcher should reach into his glove for the ball with a full hand action. If he reaches in with the grip already set, he can too easily grab the ball off center. He can also turn the ball to get a "cross-seam grip." As he moves his arm back in preparation to throw, he should try using the ring and little fingers to turn the ball.

Correct grip

Gripping the ball across the seams has proven most effective for the majority, of catchers. The two fingers are right on top of the ball. While it is not always possible to do this, by working at it, the catcher is able to grip the ball across the seams most of the time. Otherwise, he may throw sinkers or sliders, which are difficult for his teammates to handle.

A receiver should always be concerned with getting the ball out of his glove as quickly as possible.

Rather than use the webbing, one-handed catchers should try to catch the ball closer to the center of the pocket and the palm where control and feel is better. By grabbing the ball quickly and bringing the throwing hand and glove back into good throwing position, he is able to grip the ball across the seams and get rid of it more quickly.

Throwing technique

The overhand throw is not only the most accurate way to throw but is more easily handled by the receiver. The catcher's throw is made from the shoulder, and is not a complete sweep of the arm. A receiver cannot afford to wind up. His delivery must be short and quick. A catcher who gets rid of the ball quickly and accurately generally is more effective than one who throws hard but takes too long to throw.

A catcher should perfect three types of throws:

1. The full overhand throw.
2. The snap throw.
3. The sidearm flip.

To make the overhand throw, the catcher should shift his weight to his Fight foot and rotate his shoulders to the right while the ball is brought back over the right shoulder with both hands. He brings his throwing hand and mitt back together, giving him a better chance to adjust the ball in his hand. He tries to get a grip across the seams in order to give the ball the necessary backspin.

Keeping his eyes constantly on his target, the catcher cocks his arm just back of the ear and completes his throw as quickly as he can. The ball is released with a vigorous wrist and arm snap while pushing off his right foot onto his left (front) foot. The snap throw is like the full overhand throw, except that the arm is not taken back as far. This is the short and quick type of delivery. The sidearm flip is used when balls are bunted or tapped out in front of the plate, and the catcher does not have time to straighten up for the overhand throw.

Shifting and throwing

The footwork of the catcher, the manner in which he shifts his body into the throw, determines his effectiveness to a great extent. By shifting his body correctly, he will have the rhythm, power and quickness to get rid of the ball in a hurry. It is essential for the catcher to get as squarely in front of the pitch as possible in catching the ball. Knowing the steal situation, he must get as close to the batter as possible and come out into his throwing position every time.

The one-handed glove has probably spoiled catchers to the point that they do not shift their feet as much as they used to. The old-time catchers did better job of staying in front of the ball and shifting their feet. As a result, they were in better position to throw on every pitch. Catchers are becoming reluctant to shift simply because they can reach out arid backhand that ball with the one-handed glove. If they can do it, that is fine, but sometimes they get too relaxed by not shifting and some of the balls get through them. I still prefer my catchers to shift, even though they catch the ball with one hand.

On an outside pitch, by shifting and catching the ball with two hands, the catcher is in a much better position to throw the man out. By backhanding it, he has to switch the ball from there to his throwing arm and take turns getting his body into throwing position.

Crandall has an excellent theory on getting the ball away quickly. "When receiving the ball," said Del, "you do not catch the ball and then get your body in motion. If you do wait until you actually catch the ball, you are going to waste a lot of time. So, the thing to do, when you know where the ball is going and you know what you called for, get your body into motion and be ready when the ball hits the glove. Then, get it up there beside your head and throw it."

A catcher should learn to carry the ball and glove to his right ear all in one motion, adjusting the hand for the throw as it is brought up. Crandall believes, "This gets your left side in motion, and when you do turn to throw, your left side is in position; and it will bring your right side around, getting more on your throw."

"Practice going into the ball," continued Del. "It is very important not to catch the ball flatfooted. You want to be on your toes and leaning a little bit toward second base."

Types of receiving and throwing

Receiving a pitch down the middle

On a pitch over the middle of the plate, the receiver catches the ball and then steps forward with his left foot and throws. He should not move, forward to catch the ball and then throw.

Receiving an inside pitch

"We do one of two things," said Torborg. "First, he can

receive the ball and not take any steps at all, just turn and throw it. Or, he can do the same type of shuffle where he turns and throws to second base, just by having his body moving slowly through his little shuffle."

Receiving an outside pitch

On an outside pitch, with a right-handed hitter at the plate, the receiver will step right and slightly forward with his right foot, catch the ball, then step forward with his left foot for the throw to second base,

If a left-handed swinger is at the plate, and the pitch is also to the catcher's right, he again steps to the right with his right foot, catches the ball, then shifts all his weight back to his left foot. He then steps diagonally forward and toward home plate with his right foot, then forward with his left as he makes the throw. This shift will clear the batter.

"On the ball away to a right-handed hitter," said Torborg, "I just step over with the right foot, catching the ball at the same time, then stepping forward with my left foot for the throw."

Throwing technique

The catcher uses different types of footwork to receive the pitches and throw the ball quickly and accurately to the bases. While the styles of throwing differ, the fundamental techniques remain the same, both in terms of throwing technique and footwork. Young catchers' footwork, however, has to be more precise. While many big league receivers have the strength and size to make quick, snap throws, young catchers must execute proper footwork in order to get the necessary momentum and strength behind the throws.

Throwing to first base

If the pitch is away from a left-handed hitter, the catcher steps to the left with his left foot to take the pitch. His next step is forward with his right foot. Then he steps toward first base with his left foot. This action puts him in front of the hitter as he makes the throw. With a right-handed hitter at bat, the catcher should step to his left if the pitch is to his left. After the catch, he shifts his weight to the right foot, then steps out with his left foot toward first base.

On a pitch over the plate, he catches the ball and merely steps forward with the left foot for the throw to first base. If the pitch is inside to a left-handed batter, the catcher may step behind the batter for his throw. If he finds this difficult, he should step right with his right foot, make the catch, then shift his weight to his left foot, step forward with his right, then forward with his left toward first for the throw.

Throwing to second base

When throwing to second base on an inside pitch, many catchers take a lead step left and slightly forward with their left foot to receive the pitch. After getting their right foot behind their left, they step forward toward second base.

Other receivers prefer to step to the left with their left foot, catch the ball, then step forward with their right foot, shifting their weight to the right foot. Then they step forward with the left foot for the throw.

If a left-handed hitter is at bat, and the pitch is to the left of the catcher, the catcher steps to the left and, if possible, slightly forward with the left foot. The right foot is then swung behind the left or a step is taken in front of the left foot, the weight shifting to the right, and the left foot strides out for the throw. This type of shift clears the batter. The shift becomes a jump shift as it increases in speed. "Catching the ball pitched inside to a right-handed hitter can be difficult," says Torborg, unless you reach out for the ball and cup it into you.

"Catchers who use the old way step over with their left foot, step behind with the right, and then move forward on the throw Basically, that is what you still do, but you do not have time to step behind because your momentum laterally will carry you off, and you will throw with a wide open body.

"Johnny Roseboro gave me this advice on the pitch inside to a right-handed hitter: 'Catch the ball and flip your body around so that your weight is more or less on your back (right) foot, the one you push off of. You have caught the ball and you have executed the same "step-behind" footwork, However, you have kept your body down, and your shifting is similar to a crow hop. You move both your feet around, but actually, it is not a step behind because that pulls you back away from the throw to second base.'"

"While it involves the theory of stepping behind," said Jeff, "actually, it is a shuffle behind. You receive the ball and get your body into a throwing position by shifting, yet you keep your weight over your legs."

In throwing to second, the catcher should try to throw above the bag, right to the shortstop or second baseman, kneehigh, instead of trying to throw exactly to the bag. By throwing above the bag, he has a leeway. The infielder might be on the bag, and then again, if the ball is a little high, he will still be able to handle it.

Throwing to third base

With a right-handed hitter, on a pitch to his left, the catcher takes his initial step to the left and then swings his right foot diagonally backward behind his left foot. He then steps toward third base with his left foot for the throw, thus clearing the batter and going behind him.

If the pitch is away but not too wide, with the right-handed hitter still at the plate, the receiver steps to the right for the catch, then shifts his weight back to the left foot He then steps diagonally in back of the left foot, shifting his weight to the right foot, and stepping out with his left foot for the throw.

He can make this throw in front of the hitter by stepping diagonally forward with the right foot as he makes the catch. The hitter's position in the box, of course, determines the exact footwork the receiver employs. As he catches the ball, he steps either in front of or in back of the batter.

First and third steal situation

This play is used more often at the high school and college levels. A catcher should look for this play when the opponents need a run and, generally, when a weak hitter is at the plate. Defensing the double steal should be a major concern. In high school, this play is very frequent and can be devastating to the defense.

Some catchers like to make an arm fake to second, retaining the ball, and then throw quickly to third base, However, in executing this play, they take the risk of throwing the ball into left field. The simplest of signals should be used in the first and third situation. Most teams use word-of-mouth signals. If the catcher wants the pitcher to cut it off, he will tell him so as he goes halfway to the mound. Or, he may tell the pitcher to "let it go." The throw to second base has the same trajectory whether or not the pitcher cuts it off, the second baseman handles it in front of the bag or the ball goes all the way down to the base. Every player must be ready to adjust to any throwing situation.

Tagging the runner

A catcher must be aggressive when tagging a runner at the plate. If he has the ball, he must hang tough, especially if it is an important run or a "boom-boom" play. After judging the flight of the ball, the catcher should move out and place his left foot in front of home plate on the third base line. His right foot is the moving one. His heels are on the plate, and his shin guards are facing the runner.

"Let the runner see part of the plate," said Haller, "preferably the outside. This way, he has more of a tendency to use his hook slide, which is to the catcher's advantage. You might come up on the line a foot or two to receive the ball and make contact there, where he has less of a chance to get to the bag. So, let him slide in and then tag him."

"Wait for the ball to come to you," advised Tom. "Do not go out after the ball and then come back. Be on balance and mobile until you get the ball, then go into action."

As he catches the ball, the catcher turns to his left and brings his left knee down to the ground. "You do not have to reach out," said Tom, "all you have to do is make contact, with the runner. Make sure that the ball is in your glove, with your bare hand holding the ball snugly. When you make contact, just make sure that you hold on to that ball and tag him with the back into his stomach. Do not tag the runner just with the ball. Use the glove and the ball! "The easiest kind of runner to tag out is the one who goes into a hook slide. When he starts sliding, you do not have to worry about much of an impact because most of his weight is going away from you. All you have to do is go down on one knee and tag him, similar to the tag used by infielders at second or third base'.

The most important thing is for the catcher to make sure he has the ball first, and he must hold it tight, particularly on the "bang-bang" play. When he does make contact, nine times out of ten, the umpire will call the runner out because the catcher has made the contact with the runner. "The throw from right field to home can be a little more difficult," said Haller, "as well as dangerous for the catcher. Try not to get hit from the blind side. Give the runner the inside of the plate and make sure the shin guards face the runner."

The catcher should know the speed of the runner coming home, the arm of his outfielder, and the approximate distance to home plate. Normally, the catcher must have possession of the ball, or he will be called for blocking home plate. Under the heat of action, however, this is often overlooked. Obstruction, in which the catcher blocks the plate before he has the ball is very seldom called at home plate. Most catchers like to block the runner by forcing him to make an outside hook slide. They often block him a few feet from home and put the tag on him as he scrambles for the plate.

"The catcher should make the runner commit

himself first, and then he counters," said Haller. "Remember, the runner has his momentum built up. Therefore, the catcher should put his left foot right on the base line, and if he hooks, he will hook right into that shin guard."

Forcing the runner

With the bases loaded and the throw coming into the plate from an infielder, the catcher has the assignment of forcing the runner and trying for the double play at first base. On a good throw, the catcher places his right foot on the plate. As he catches the ball, he steps forward with his left foot, and throws to first base. Throws that are received wide of the plate are caught by stepping to the side on which the ball is thrown.

"Make sure the throw is to you," advised Tom, "that your foot is on the plate. Sometimes, you do not know how much time you have, but make sure you get the first out. Then, as you step toward first base, try to keep the ball inside of the runner so the first baseman can handle the ball easily." In throwing to the first baseman on a possible double play, the receiver must be sure to get clearance from home plate. If not, he could get racked up by the runner, and his throw might end up down the right field corner.

Catching the pop fly

Most big-league catchers like to catch pop flies with their back to the infield; because of the rotation of the baseball, the ball usually comes back toward the infield. This is known as the infleld drift, and the catcher must allow for it. The higher the foul ball, the more drift it will take, which can be as much as three to five feet. This is what makes pop foul balls hard to catch. Experience is most important in catching high pop-ups, and it comes only after handling many pop flies during practice and games. In doing so, the catcher can build up the necessary confidence. Catching pop-ups is a matter of practice and allowing for the rotation of the ball.

" The more you catch," said Haller, "the more you know when the foul pop-up is in play, just by the sound of the ball. If a ball goes over your right shoulder, you should then turn to your right, and vice versa if the ball goes over your left shoulder."

The high pop-up hit directly over home plate is particularly difficult to catch. After judging the ball, the catcher throws his mask away and moves into the ball. His back is toward the infield. "Many catchers will go out and have the ball come back into them," said Haller "Then, there are those who will stay there, and move out facing the infield. They know the ball will move out, and then they will overplay it somewhat, and the ball will come out in front of them.',

If the pop-up is moving into the infield away from the plate, one of the infielders should handle the catch. The catcher should go after every pop-up until he is called off by either the third baseman or the first baseman, either of whom might have a better angle and a better shot at it. The pitcher plays an important role in these situations. As soon as he realizes who should catch the ball, he yells the last name of the player, and his teammates can react accordingly.

After getting a good sight on the ball and judging its return, the catche should be sure to throw his mask in an opposite direction. He should avoid turning around too much,

"Most of the balls are usually away from the plate," explained Tom. "So you do not have to worry about stepping on your mask. On those balls hi directly overhead, you should hold on to your mask for a moment and discard it to either side, depending on which way you have to move.

Catching the ball

Most catchers point their gloves upward when catching the pop-up. This technique is similar to that used by outfielders, with the hand and glove up at about eye-level, with the fingers of the glove pointed up. "I prefer the other method," stated Haller, "with the hands close to my belt and opened up.

Fielding bunts

In fielding bunts, the catcher must move out after the ball as quickly as possible. He has to get a good jump on the ball. The speed of his moves will depend, of course, on how fast the batter is running down to first base. If he is a real fast runner, it could be a desperation play If he is only an average runner, he will have more time to get set and throw him out. "Try to field all rolling bunts with two hands," advised Haller. "Placing your glove out in front of the ball, you want to scoop the ball into your glove with the throwing hand. Do it all in one motion and make sure you have good control of the ball. Never take your eyes off the ball!"

In throwing, some catchers like to come back over the top, while some prefer to throw sidearm. If it is a hurry situation, they have to throw from their fielding position and make a quick, sidearm throw. The bare hand should be used only if the ball has stopped rolling and it is a "do-or-die" play.

Down the third base line

There are two theories on fielding the bunt down the third base line. Most catchers prefer to turn their back to first base and approach the ball as quickly as possible, rather than take the time to circle the ball. It is generally believed to be faster for the receiver to turn his back on the play. Others like to circle the ball, since this method helps keep the play in front of them at all times.

Foot-and whirl method

On a rolling ball, the catcher places his left foot as close to the ball as possible, allowing him plenty of room to field it as it rolls to his right If the ball stops rolling, he places his right foot close to the ball and makes a turn to his left on his right foot, then steps out with his left foot as he throws to first base.

The primary task is to place the glove in front of the ball to stop it. As he pivots his right foot, he uses his glove to flip the ball into his throwing hand. As he fields the ball, his right foot, is placed ahead of his left foot, thus down his angle in turning around for the throw.

Circling the ball

Some catchers like to have the play in front of them at all times, circling to the left of the ball, if possible. "I prefer circling the ball because I can snap the ball to first base as fast and hard as I can in turning and pivoting around," said Haller. "While it takes another step as far as the runner is concerned, I think it is the surest way You always have everything in front of you. If the throw is to go to second base, I do not circle as much."

Down the first base line

The catcher should move out as quickly as possible, buff the ball with his glove, take one step with his right foot, step with his left foot, and throw sidearm to the first baseman. He remains low to the ground when fielding and throwing, and by keeping the play in front of him, he should be able to make an accurate throw to the first baseman.

Run-down play

On a run-down situation occurring between home and third, if he has the ball, the catcher should run the base runner as hard as he can toward third base. When the runner is about halfway down the line, he should bring his throwing arm to the area of the shoulder. As soon as the third baseman moves into the play, he should toss him the ball about chest-high, with the receiver placing the tag on the runner. One throw should be all that is necessary.

After the toss, the catcher should get out of the way to his outside and go back. The catcher and third baseman must be on the inside of the base runner, keeping the runner on one side. They should never let him bisect their view or throwing procedure. Catchers, like infielders, are advised not to make more than one fake throw.

Covering and backing up

Whenever a ground ball is hit to the infielders with no

runners on base, the catcher should move quickly down the first base line in foul territory, and back up the first baseman. Generally, he runs parallel to and about thirty-five or forty feet from the line as fast as he can. When the first baseman goes after a short fly ball, the catcher often covers first base. He also covers third base when a bunt of slowly hit ball is fielded by the third baseman with only first base occupied.

Cutoffs

If the throw from the outfield is accurate and if the catcher does not want the infielder to cut the ball off, he should remain silent. However, in an exciting game with plenty of noise, he will often yell, "Leave it alone," or "Let it go!" If he wants the infielder to cut the ball and make a play, he will yell, "Cut." The catcher will yell, "Relay" if the throw coming into home is to be cut off and thrown home.

Working with the pitcher

The catcher must call the game according to the type of pitcher with whom he is working. In sizing up a hitter, a catcher, above all, must remember his pitcher's ability, even more so than the hitter's weakness. It is particularly important to work more around the pitcher's strength if the catcher does not have a "book" on the hitter.

The type of control his pitcher has will be a big factor in what pitches the catcher will call. He does not want to get his pitcher in a hole. He should want the pitcher to work in front as much as possible. Therefore, he should try to go with pitches of which he knows the pitcher has good control.

If his fast ball is good on a particular day, he might start out with a fast ball. But he must mix up the balls, especially with some off-speed pitches. Otherwise, the hitter will learn just what to expect. The big thing is to *get ahead of the hitter* and work from that point. In a tough situation, the catcher should call for the strongest pitch that his pitcher has on the particular day. Just because the hitter is weak on a curve does not necessarily mean to throw him curves, unless the pitcher can throw a good curve ball. If he has a poor curve, perhaps it would be best to waste that pitch, or merely "show" the curve. Quite often, what is effective for one pitcher may not be effective for a other. A letup pitch on a 3-1 count can be a good call for some pitchers and will often force the hitter to hit the ball with his timing slightly off.

On 3-1, as well as 2-0 situations, many catchers will call for an "off " pitch. This pitch, though, must be a strike, preferably low and away. The pitcher wants the hitter to hit this ball, not miss it, hoping, of course, that the batter's timing will be off.

Studying the hitters

The pitcher and catcher must make a thorough study of the opposing hitters and freely discuss them together. They should study the hitter's stance and remember what pitch he went for and where he hit the ball in previous appearances. Batting practice is a good time to watch the opposing hitters. It does not take long to find out who the pull hitters are, those who hit straightaway, and the opposite field swingers.

However, young battery combinations are advised not to worry too much about stances and batting positions. After they get ahead of the hitter, though, they could consider his stance and his relationship to the plate. If the batter crouches over the plate, the catcher should advise his pitcher to keep the ball high and inside. The batter who steps away from the plate should be pitched outside, while the hitter who stands up straight should be given pitches down low. Some hitters crowd the plate, because they want the tight pitch. Those who stand far from the plate invite the outside pitch.

Setting up a hitter

Setting up a hitter to make him hit the pitcher's best pitch is very important. However, to a large extent, this depends on the control of the pitcher.

Going out to the mound

When going out to the mound, the catcher should have something definite to say to the pitcher. Some pitchers need a few harsh words to get them going. The catcher might have to make them a little angry at times. Other pitchers may need a pat on the back and a few words of encouragement. More than likely, if a pitcher runs into control trouble, he is basically high and usually is doing one of two things wrong. First, he could be rushing, which would cause him to be high with his pitches. "We usually look for this, and if we see it," said Haller, "we will go out and talk to him and say, 'You are rushing. Stay back and don't rush the delivery.'

"If you pinpoint one or two things wrong, very likely it will settle him down. Pitchers have a tough job. The biggest job is to concentrate for nine innings. Quite often, when a pitcher gets in trouble, he is not concentrating enough on what he wants to do."

Sometimes it is effective for the catcher to go out and talk to his pitcher just to slow him do" a little. A little humour or a joke might be good at this time to help him relax.

Relationship with umpires

In their relationship with umpires, catchers generally fall into three groups:

1. The catcher who lets the umpire know that he has missed a pitch.
2. The receiver who argues on every close pitch called against his pitcher.
3. The one who does not say a word, and gives the impression that he is not in the ball game.

We like our catchers to practice more the first point listed. When a catcher is sure the umpire missed the call, he should, without turning around, let him know that he has missed his pitch. In our league, a catcher is not allowed to turn around and argue with him. If he misses another one, he has to raise hell again, but within reason, of course. The catcher has to be sure that he is right " though, before he makes too big an argument about it.

Crandall had this to say about his relationship with umpires: "I did not particularly like to argue with umpires, but when I thought I was right, I had my words. If a catcher feels that he is right, he has to say something because, if he does not, the umpires will feel he is not in the ball game. Then they might get a little careless. I am not saying they do not bear down all the time—they do but I know as a player, if the manager did not get on me once in a while, I would get a little careless, and I think the same thing goes for umpires."

" I believe you should have a cordial relationship with umpires," said Haller. "To have their respect, you must respect them. As long as I know that he is consistent, that he is that way all the time, I do not often get disturbed. But I do not like to see a fellow changing his mind all the time. For one hitter, he will call a particular pitch a ball, and then for the next hitter, he might call the same pitch a strike. This can be very disturbing to me. Generally, though, in our league our umpires are very consistent.

"Being a habitual griper can hurt you more than it can help you," Haller believes. "You do not get many birds with salt. You get a lot more out there if you try to butter them up. If you want the respect of umpires, do not try to show them up. Then they will have a little more respect for you."

Drills for catchers

One-step drill

This is an excellent drill for catchers who take too many steps and overdo their footwork In this drill, the catcher receives the ball with his weight already on his right foot, steps with his left, and throws.

Footwork warm-up drill

This is a drill to be used just prior to infield practice, in which the catcher uses correct footwork in shifting for the throw. He and another catcher play "hard" catch from a distance of sixty-five to seventy-five feet, in which they execute the same shifting footwork they will use during the game.

Throwing drill

Practice catching low throws with full equipment on.

Rules in working on the hitter

I. Find out as soon as possible which pitch is working best.
2. Always try to get *ahead* of the batter. Get that first ball over for a strike.
3. Watch the hitter's position in the box, and call your pitches accordingly.
4. Make a thorough study of opposing hitters, and discuss them freely with the pitcher.
5. If the pitcher is wild, slow him down occasionally.
6. Call for pitches that will throw a batter off his timing or fool him.
7. Never get beaten in a tight situation on a pitch that is not the pitcher's best pitch.

Basic catching rules

1. Be the field general, and direct the play on all batted balls.
2. Keep check on the defensive positions of the infielders and outfielders.
3. Give the pitcher a good target at all times, crouching low.
4. On the intentional pass, keep one foot in the catcher's box until the pitcher releases the ball.
5. Learn the most effective pitch for every hurler you handle.

6. Talk to your pitcher!
7. Be alert for any possible steal or hit-and-run play. A pitchout may be called.
8. Back up first base with the bases unoccupied on all batted balls that might result in overthrows.
9. On throws from the outfield, call "CUT" to the cutoff man if a throw to the plate is wide, or if the runner cannot be retired.
10. If the bunt is in order, have your pitcher pitch high.
11. Study the hitter's stance, and remember what he went after, and where he hit the ball in previous appearances.

4 BATTING

Ball players have a natural tendency to try to hit every pitch out of the park. As a result, they swing too hard, adversely affecting timing, level swing, stride, thinking, and everything that goes toward making solid contact. I firmly believe that if hitters concentrated on making good contact, they would hit more home runs. Players will be surprised at how hard they can hit the ball using a short stroke. A good, quick swing is the secret to good hitting. By shortening the stride and stroke of the bat, a hitter can compensate for the off-speed pitches and get better contact and better wood on the ball than he can by taking a long swing and a long, lunging stride. Unless a hitter has good bat control, he is not going to be a consistent hitter. He has to put the bat on the ball!

"The quickest way for a ball player to become a good hitter," advised Johnny Pesky, hitting coach of the Boston Red Sox, "is to concentrate more on trying to meet the ball and to hit the ball where it is pitched. Choking up and taking a shorter swing will help assure the bat control that is necessary to hit the ball to all fields."

Effective hitting

Major league batting coaches are in firm agreement in

advocating a relaxed, smooth, rhythmic swing that stresses proper alignment of the head, perfect balance, and full arm extension. Indeed, this type of hitting swing enables a batter to hit the ball hard more consistently than does a crowd-the-plate, arms-in, tense, muscle-up, swing-from-the-heels approach. Hitting the ball hard is more important than is hitting it to a particular field. If you hit the ball hard consistently, the base hits will take care of themselves. "When I try to pull, I have a tendency to jerk my head off the ball," said Steve Garvey, who has combined power with his ability to hit the ball to all fields. "Generally, I will go with the pitch."

The good hitter is aggressive. We like to see a batter up at the plate who will attack the ball, one who is always going into the ball. We encourage our hitters to go get the ball. They cannot let the ball get in on them too quickly. A nonaggressive hitter is one who more or less lays back and just feels for the ball. Rod Carew, seven-time American League batting champion, is always thinking, "it doesn't matter what the pitch is, I'll get my cut at it!" While he must be aggressive, the batter should not lunge into the ball. Rather, we prefer him to take a short, casual stride into the pitch, allowing him to keep his body back. If his body moves out in front too quickly, the hitter will have a difficult time adjusting to the pitch. Consequently, he will lose power in his swing. He should take a stride that allows him to glide into the swing, rather than jump into it, resulting in a smooth stride.

Quickness with the hands and wrists is a most important phase of hitting. The ability to be quick with the hands, wrists, and arms will determine just how good a hitter a player is going to be. If a hitter is fast with his hands and wrists, he will be able to wait longer for the pitch. How can a hitter become quicker with his hands and wrists? To get more bat speed, he has to develop more strength. While there are many good strength exercises, I think the best way to improve arm strength is to get a bat eight or ten ounces heavier than the one the hitter uses in the game and swing it, and keep on swinging it! The only way to become a good hitter is to swing the bat constantly, not just when taking the few swings in batting practice. It is the desire to hit and the willingness to practice that makes great hitters. While not every boy can become a great hitter, every player can improve through instruction and practice.

Perhaps the most important rules in batting are a level swing, timing, and hitting the ball where it is pitched. A level swing provides the greatest hitting arc--to hit the ball where it is pitched. Outside pitches should be hit to the opposite field, while inside pitches should be pulled. With the improved change of speeds and different pitches being thrown today, timing is probably the biggest factor in hitting. Only constant work at the plate, swinging at every type of pitch, will give a hitter timing.

What is the proper swing?

The type of swing depends on the hitter himself and, of course, on where the ball is pitched. The arc of swing varies--level, slightly upward, or slightly downward. Each hitter must develop his own style to meet his physical abilities, such as power and speed. On the low ball, the batter has to come up; otherwise, he will hit the ball on the ground. On the high pitch, he has to take a slightly downward stroke at the ball. A hitter will generally start the swing downward, but finish with a little uppercut. Actually, the bat starts down and then levels off through the swing. On the point of contact the swing is fairly level. The follow-through will be a slightly upward swing, especially if the hitter turns loose with the top hand and lets the bottom hand get good extension.

"The important point is to eliminate a loop," said Charlie Lau, batting coach of the Chicago White Sox. "If you keep the bat head above your hands, you will eliminate a loop. A pitcher loves to see that little loop, and can find it very easily." An increasing number of hitting instructors are emphasizing the "slightly downward swing," the chop or slap type of swing in which the hitter shortens up and swings down slightly.

"The reason why we tell our hitters to swing down slightly," says Dick Sisler, former batting coach of the St. Louis Cardinals, "is to more or less go to the extreme to make them level off we think that if a hitter will level off on a high pitch, he will hit the ball on a line more." Then, there is Ted Williams, who prefers to stress "the slightly upward swing." Ted, who was one of the game's truly great hitters with the Boston Red Sox, believes that "a hitter can generate more power this way than he can swinging down on the pitch."

Most home run hitters have a slight uppercut, which is all right for a player with good power; but for the majority of hitters, I stress the level swing and have them put more weight forward to prevent uppercutting. Spray hitters, those who hit to all fields, should use a heavier bat, choke up, and try to make contact. They will find that the ball will come off the bat more sharply than if they use a lighter bat. Generally, I like to see our hitters stress line drives at all times. True, a batter will hit a percentage of the balls on the ground, and he will hit a percentage of fly balls. However, I feel that by concentrating on going to the line drive he is more apt to make good contact consistently.

Select a bat you can control

The weight of the bat is very important. Each player must decide for himself what type of bat is right for him. He should find one that feels good in his hands, neither too heavy nor too light. The bat has to feel comfortable to him. There is no certain size bat for any particular individual. A coach should fit the bat to the individual, taking into consideration the size of his hands and his physical abilities. It should be more or less a feet. A hitter should pick up a bat, balance it, and determine whether he likes the feel of the handle, whether or not it feels good in his hands. The bat's weight should also be considered.

Many hitters have found success with the lighter and thinner bats, with the weight out on the hitting area. The idea behind using this type of bat is to swing the bat faster, thereby getting more velocity into the swing. When the bat is too light, however, a hitter has a tendency to overswing, to swing too hard. With a heavier bat, the hitter has better control, and with more wood, he has a greater chance of hitting the ball. For the majority of hitters, a heavier bat choked up for balance is more effective than a light bat swung from the end.

Even though John Bench is a power hitter, he uses a bat considered fairly light by major league standards:

thirty-five and half inches long and weighing between thirty-two and thirty-three ounces.

Assume a comfortable stance

The stances used by successful major league hitters vary. A batter should move his feet around until he finds a stance that feels good. The best stance is the most comfortable one. As he assumes his position at the plate, the hitter should make sure he has complete coverage of the plate. He should be close enough to the plate to handle pitches on the outside corner and far enough from the inside corner to keep from being handcuffed or jammed on the fists. In general, the long ball hitter employs a wide stance, while the batter who likes to drive or punch the ball through or over the infield uses a narrow one. Some hitters vary their stance against certain pitchers. They move up in the box against breaking ball pitchers and move deeper against fast ball pitchers.

Basically, we like to start a young hitter out with both of his feet even, not closed, not open, and adjust from there. The most balanced position is one with the feet shoulder-width apart, and with the front foot turned a little toward the pitcher. The weight is distributed equally on the balls of the feet.

The head must be held fairly still. It has to move a little, but very little. It is like a good golf swing. Both eyes should be facing the pitcher and the ball. A hitter should move his eyes to watch the ball, but never move his head. The hips and shoulders must be kept level, with the front hip and shoulder pointing at the pitcher. If a player maintains level hips and shoulders while swinging, he will very likely take a level swing, keeping his hands about chest height and above the toes of his rear foot. He should tuck the chin in close to the front shoulder to keep his head from pulling away as he swings. Some hitters believe they see the ball better when they keep their eyes level as they watch the ball. A hitter who is a little slow with the bat should open up the stance. One who cannot handle the outside pitch, should try hitting from a closed stance and getting closer to the plate. A closed stance is effective against breaking pitches because it enables a hitter to hang in there a little better. "Stance is really not that important," said Johnny Pesky, who compiled a lifetime batting average of .307 with the Red Sox. "Various stances can be used. I advocate the closed stance because we believe that the bat stays in better position with this stance, and the bat does not move quite as far. Most of the good hitters used a closed stance--Musial, Williams, and down the line." Whatever stance he uses, a hitter must be comfortable in the batter's box. If a hitter has a tendency to pull away from the ball, he should consider placing a little more weight on the front foot. He should keep the bat cocked back, and the front shoulder in.

Tension can be a real problem to a hitter. The solution to tension at the plate is some kind of rhythmic movement before the swing--a slight bend in the knees, shuffling of the feet, or a waggle of the hips. The movement helps the hitter relax. It is particularly important to bend the knees when hitting the curve ball. The hitter who is too stiff in the legs always has difficulty hitting breaking pitches.

The batter must keep his hips under him. If his hips and butt stick out too far, he 'will be on his heels, rather than the balls of the feet He can move more quickly and maintain better control of his body if he starts in a relaxed position rather than a tense one. I do not like to see hitters bent over too much, since this position makes them stiff.

Grip

The grip of the batter should be comfortable and firm but not tense and tight The hitter should grip the bat where he can swing it best. He can do this by "shaking hands" with the bat and lining up the middle knuckles of both hands. Most hitters align the second and third knuckles with a flat surface of the two hands. This grip places the middle knuckle of the top hand somewhere between the middle and last knuckle of the bottom hand for better wrist snap. The hands should be close together. A loose, relaxed grip is essential for quickness and power. A tight grip has a tendency to tighten up the forearm muscles and the biceps. While assuming a relaxed position at the plate, the hitter should have a firm grip with his bottom hand and a loose grip with his top hand.

"As far as the top hand is concerned," said Joe Torre, an outstanding hitter in the National League before becoming a manager, "the bat should not be squeezed but held loosely, in the fingers rather than in the palm, which enables the hitter to turn his wrists better at impact This type of grip allows him to be freer and to 'pop the bat' into the ball."

Then, as he throws the bat at the ball on the swing, the batter should tighten up his grip. So, he must remember to relax until he is ready to actually swing. He keeps his grip loose, but as he starts swinging, the hands and wrists tighten, providing maximum power at the right time.

The hitter should hold his bat in the "ready" position that is comfortable for him. I urge my players to hold their hands about chest height because that is where the high pitch is going to be. If the ball is above their hands, they are urged to take it. If it is below their hands, they should "jump" on it. This gives a player a better idea of the strike zone. Most hitters hold their hands approximately letter-high, and just slightly behind their rear leg. True, hitters like Carl Yastrzemski and Fred Lynn keep their hands even higher, but they have to come down to swing.

Position in the box

Most hitters prefer to stand about even with the plate. A hitter has to be close enough to control the outside part. By touching the outside corner with his bat, the batter can tell whether he is close enough to have full coverage of the plate. Some fellows think it is better to stand in the back of the box, giving them more time to look at the pitch. One disadvantage, however, in being in the extreme end of the box is that a breaking pitch will break even bigger back there. In other words, the ball gets the full sweep of its break toward the plate there. The farther away a hitter stands from the plate on a curve ball, the bigger break he has to take care of while covering the plate.

"Many of the major league hitters hit from the back of the box, close to the catcher," observed Wally Moses, for many years an outstanding hitter and batting coach. "I like a hitter who is more even with the plate." "I think the hitter is better off hitting a curve ball as it is breaking in, rather than after it breaks. Therefore, the sooner he can catch it, the better off he will be, before it breaks bigger," said Johnny

Sain, a great pitching coach and exponent of the breaking ball.

"Most of the young hitters have a tendency to crowd the plate," according to Ted Williams. "That, to me, is the hardest way of all to hit. If I crowd the plate, my hands and arms extend over to the inside corner of the plate, and in order for me to hit it, I have to get my bat out well in front of the plate. Because I am so close to the plate, I have to hit the ball well out in front of the plate, allowing me less time to hit the ball squarely on the meat of the bat. "Now, in order to become a good hitter, the quicker you can be, the more time you give yourself," continued Williams. "So, in order to get more time and be fooled less, simply move away from the plate, approximately ten inches to a foot.

Know the strike zone

Knowledge of the strike zone is an important aspect of hitting. The more selective a hitter is in swinging at pitches, the easier it will be for him to develop into a good hitter. Once pitchers find he is going to swing at bad pitches, he will get very little else.

A baseball, thrown with great speed and plenty of stuff on it, is tough enough to hit even when it is in the strike zone. When a hitter goes after bad pitches, out of the strike zone, he makes his job much more difficult The strike zone is an area the width of the plate and extending from the knees to slightly under the armpits.

Watch the ball: Picking up the ball is very important to a hitter. Good hitters see the ball longer than do poor hitters. As soon as the ball is released, the batter has to pick up the spin. He should be able to tell by the way the ball is rotating whether the pitch is a fast ball or a curve. "Pitchers tend to throw curves more overhand," explained Rod Carew. "They get on top of the ball. As a result, the ball has a great amount of overhand spin. A fast ball doesn't have that much rotation, and a slider comes in at a three-quarter angle."

A hitter should follow the ball right into the catcher's glove. He should never take his eyes off the ball, even if he doesn't swing at it.

"I try to hit the ball up the middle," said Carew. "If you look to left or right field, to where you want to hit the ball, you're cutting down on your concentration. You can't look at left or right field and at the pitcher, too. That's why we try to hit the ball to center. That way, I'm looking at the field I'm aiming for, I'm looking right at the pitcher, and I'm not swinging too early in an attempt to pull the ball."

Wait on the pitch

The good hitter is a waiter. He gets that last extra look. The better he is at watching the pitch as it comes toward him, the longer he can wait before swinging. Hitters with good wrists and hands can wait until the last split-second and then whip the bat forward with power as well as authority.

Patience is one of the most important qualities for a hitter. To hit the ball well, a hitter must wait until it gets to the plate and then rip into it. Take a real good look at the pitch, and then hit it! The hitter should try to keep from watching the body motion or eccentric moves of pitchers. If he follows their pumps or motions too closely, he may be attracted to something other than the ball, such as a high leg or a jerky shoulder movement.

To be a good waiter, the hitter must have quick reflexes, quick hands and wrists, and excellent eye and muscle coordination.

The hitting swing

A level, natural swing is a characteristic of all batting champions. The younger hitter, particularly, should just go for the line drive and let the home runs take care of themselves. He should always try to meet the ball solidly, and not try to overswing. By making good contact, a batter always has a chance for a hit. The shorter and more compact the swing, the better chance a hitter has for contact. This is the secret of hitting.

The good swing is as level as possible. Naturally, the type of swing depends on where the ball is pitched. On the low pitch the hitter does come up on his swing. He has to come up. In fact, most hitters uppercut slightly. It is perfectly natural to swing up on a low pitch. However, if he uppercuts pitches across his letters or high pitches, the hitter will have a lot of trouble. These are the pitches on which he must swing slightly down, particularly with a hard Meld and if the hitter has good speed afoot. The swing is somewhat of a chopping one.

"I recommend a short, compact swing," said Pete Rose, one of baseball's greatest hitters. "I like to see a hitter go up there and swing hard and just hit the ball. The top hitters in baseball use different swings. Carew's swing, for example, is flat, while Reggie Smith's is high, but the key is that when the front foot comes down, the bat is either off or behind the back leg. The secret is to coordinate the parts of the hitting swing into perfect unison, which requires perfect timing. *Timing is the key to the hitting game.*

Taking a rather short stride

Short stride keeps the hitter's body balanced and enables him to have split-second timing. In addition, the short stride allows him to check a swing if the pitch is bad. The player who takes a short step controls his forward motion. He is not only properly balanced, but he is able to focus his eyes better on the ball. He can wait longer on the ball, and then he can adjust to the pitch.

"I take a short stride," said Pete Rose, "because it helps me keep my weight on my back foot. But there are hitters like Johnny Bench and Henry Aaron who prefer a longer stride. When I take a long stride, I have a tendency to start lunging, so I keep my stride to four to six inches." For many hitters, though, a four to six inch stride is not realistic. Jerry Kindall points out that, "Most good hitters stride twice that in game situations."

The purpose of the stride is to force the weight onto the rear foot and keep it there until the swing is started. The body weight must never be ahead of the swing. Motion pictures show that a batter hits the ball a fraction of a second after the stride.

We find that batters who stride longer are getting ready too quickly, this causes them to become lunge hitters. Consequently, the hitter goes out too quickly to meet the ball, and the only thing he is using to hit is his arms. Essentially, if he can stay back and wait and take a short stride, the batter will have the compact swing necessary for successful hitting.

If he finds he has to overstride and that he cannot cut his stride down, a player should try to hold his bat back until the pitcher gets the ball on the way. If he does not commit his bat with his front foot, he can take a big. stride, as long as he does not start his bat with his foot. By taking a short stride, the hitter can more or less just shift his weight from the back to the front foot. The front foot that he~ hits into is firm.

By striding in, a hitter will likely keep that front shoulder in and not open up too quickly. He will not make as many mistakes on the breaking ball. Schmidt credits an adjustment he made at the plate in 1980 with making him a better hitter. "I began standing off the plate and striding into the ball a little more.

The casual stride

We like a hitter to take a short, "casual stride," simply because it allows him to keep his body back. The "casual stride" is not a lunge. It is more of a lifting or shifting of the weight from both feet to a little more on the back foot. The front or striding foot is more or less free to just take the "casual stride" into the pitch.

The casual stride enables the hitter to stride forward with his front foot but not let his body go forward. The weight of the body is kept back, and the bat is back. Although he has taken the same length of stride, the player has held his body back, and his bat is back~ cocked, and ready to meet the ball when it comes. He is on balance, as he is throughout the swing.

Weight shift Weight shift is very important to hitting success, There are many ways in which hitters transfer their weight forward. A good extension of the arms will result in a good weight shift. At the point of contact, the front leg is as rigid as a board.'

Batting authorities differ in their interpretation of the weight shift on the hitting swing. The high-speed sequence films of the great hitters through the years demonstrate that a baseball hitter has to hit against a firm front side, a closed front hip. To obtain a controlled stride, it is essential to maintain a firm rear foot because a hitter gene rates his power in his push forward as he "throws the bat" at the ball.

Many of the great hitters of baseball used a short stride because it kept their body balanced and helped them have split-second timing. The batter who takes a short step controls his forward motion. He is able to stay properly balanced.

Cocking action When the front foot comes down, the hands are back behind and off the back leg, ready to trigger the swing forward. The back elbow is normally kept down, not up. The hitter feels comfortable at the plate. He has his bat back and his wrists cocked as he looks at the pitcher over his front shoulder. In this position, the hitter is ready to accelerate forward. The raised back elbow has been used by a number of hitting greats, including Joe DiMaggio, Ted Williams, and, more recently, Fred Lynn and Carl Yastrzemski. The elbow-up position does add power and distance, but it can reduce consistency and good contact. Batters who hit with the back elbow up, however, are less prone to hitch than are those who hit with the back elbow down. If a hitter is slow with the bat, he generally should not raise his elbow. Before the start of the swing, there is a little movement of the hands. The great hitters use a little "cocking" action. As the batter gets ready for the pitch, the hands move slightly up, rather than down and then up.

Keep a strong front arm

A hitter has to use his front arm correctly. The front arm more or less guides the swing, and then the top hand does a little snapping. Unfortunately, many hitters fail to use the front arm properly, one reason being that they are weak in the triceps muscle, which is responsible for "whipping the front arm out" Therefore, a hitter must build up those muscles which will give him this bat speed: the muscles in the back of the arm. The triceps muscle in the back of the arm, which throws the bat out at the ball, is the one to be built up. Unfortunately, quite a few hitters get their top hand in too quickly and begin rolling their wrists when the ball is fairly even with them. Some batters use their top hand too much, and fail to use the front arm enough.

He must really push his shoulder toward the pitcher. If the batter does not drive the shoulder toward the ball, his head will move and he will lose sight of the ball. Many hitters tend to let their front shoulder pull out just a fraction too early. This causes them to pull their body away just enough to get the ball on the end of the bat. Instead, the hitter should tuck his chin in close to his front shoulder to keep the shoulder from pulling out too early.

Rotating the hips

As well as from the wrists and arms, batting power comes from rotating the hips. According to many hitting experts, the action of the hips is more responsible for a powerful swing than is the roll of the wrists and hands. Getting the hips out of the way and letting the momentum and power of the body come forward into the swing is one of the most important points in hitting. The batter who hits from a closed stance and with locked hips must try to open up, in order to get his hips out of the way. Good wrists and hands are essential because they "pop the ball" well, but on contact with the ball the hands are still fairly straight and the wrist turn-over occurs afterward, like a follow-through which provides the extra pop. So, it all comes back to the power of the hips. A hitter has to put his hips, into it!

For good hip rotation, the rear foot must turn to face toward the pitcher. The turn forces the front hip to open up. When the back foot turns, there is no way that a hitter can stop the front hip from opening. The hips open up to give the hitter room for his hands to come through and to bring the hands in for the tight pitch. In turning, the hitter is transferring his weight forward. The hitter has to hit against a firm front side, a closed front hip. He actually opens up before he swings, but he should start his swing against a firm front hip. Throwing the bat then pulls the hitter in behind the ball. He pivots on the back foot, with a relaxed, bent knee. He pushes vigorously forward with his back foot.

Good hip rotation produces bat speed. Paul Waner, like his brother, a great hitter with the Pittsburgh Pirates, called it "the quick belly button." By "the quick belly button," he meant speed in the rotation of the hips. The manner in which the bat is thrown out makes the batter quick in the hips, gives him a quick pivot.

Quickness with the hands and wrists

Being quick with the hands and wrists is one of the most important phases of hitting. "The quicker they are as the ball comes to the plate," explained Williams, "the longer you can wait to judge the pitcher, and the less you will be fooled." Once the hitter decides to pull the trigger, he must get his bat moving quickly Everything--shoulders, hips, hands, and wrists--is brought through smoothly, unleashing his full power on the ball. The wrist snap is the final accelerator after the hips, shoulders, forearms, and hands have laid the bat on the ball.

For years, many baseball authorities were erroneously stating that the hitter breaks his wrists when the bat is across the plate. Wally Moses, in refuting this theory, said that "a hitter should hit the ball before he breaks his wrists." The head of the bat is what turns the wrists over. Again, the ball should be met in front of the plate, just before the hitter breaks his wrists. Quite a few hitters, incorrectly, bring their top hand in too quickly and begin rolling their wrists when the ball is fairly even with them. Instead, a hitter should hit the ball before he breaks his wrists.

Just at impact, and slightly afterward, the hitter's wrists start breaking, and then comes the smooth follow-through. The wrists break just after contact with the ball, to give the swing that extra punch that sends the ball well on its way.

Full extension of the arms

The batter's hands start from the top, about shoulder high, are thrown right out in front, and then move on through. As contact with the ball is made, the arms are fully extended and the eyes remain on the ball. The batter hits the ball as the front arm becomes straight.

Power hitters such as Mike Schmidt and Jack

Clark like to keep their arms away from their bodies to give greater arm extension. The hitter who holds the bat too close to the body may have difficulty getting the arms out when he swings, causing too much roll of the hands and wrists. A dominant or strong top hand can prevent a full-arm extension by taking over after contact and causing too much roll of the hands and wrists. To prevent this roll, hitting coaches such as Lau advocate releasing the top hand after driving through and making contact with the ball.

Popping the top hand is where a hitter really gets the turnover of his wrists. He should pull with his left or bottom hand, which will help him extend his arms in hitting, and then pop with the right.

Follow-through

After the hips and wrists have whipped through and hit the ball, a complete follow-through is necessary. A complete follow-through provides power to the swing and gives distance to the hits. The body follows through in the direction the ball is hit, and the bat continues under its own momentum to the rear of the body. The wrists snap and roll over. The arms swing to the rear. The hitter should be in perfect balance, with the body facing the direction of the ball just hit.

A batter should never stop or "chop off" his swing. When he completes his swing, his bat should be at the middle of his back. The rear hip follows through. The belt buckle comes around and faces left field on an inside pitch, center on a pitch down the middle, and right on an outside pitch. The weight comes forward, causing the back foot to pivot, or, for some hitters, to lift on contact with the pitch.

While some hitters have their rear foot off the ground, the lifting comes only after they have made contact with the ball. To obtain a controlled stride, it is essential to maintain a firm rear foot because a hitter generates his power in his push forward as he throws the bat at the ball.

Proper mental approach

The ability to think at home plate is important What is the pitcher throwing? What is his, best pitch? What did he get me out on last time? What am I going to do? One of the best things any hitter can do when he is up at the plate is to concentrate on the pitcher and try to imagine that every pitch is coming into the strike zone and he is going to put the bat on the ball. He must have confidence in himself, a positive feeling that he can do it! He has to have a mental attitude that says, "I know I can do it."

Above all, a hitter has to be as relaxed as possible. He cannot react quickly enough or take a smooth swing if his muscles are tight. He should not get set too soon. He should wait until the pitcher is "ready" to pitch before he gets into his ready position.

Relaxation is essential to becoming a good hitter. Actually, concentration and relaxation go together in hitting a baseball. By concentrating on what he is doing, a player can remove tension and fear from his mind and substitute the all-important vehicles to success--a confident mind and a relaxed body

"In hitting, the element of fear has to be eliminated," said Charlie Lau. "A hitter has to go out on his front foot and get that ball. Subconsciously a hitter doesn't realize that he is pulling away from the ball. A lot of hitters are rocking back away from the ball, and they don't know it Instead, he must go out on his front foot and attack that ball!" One good ay to help a hitter to overcome fear at the plate is to throw him tennis balls instead of baseballs in betting practice. He will gain confidence when he realizes he is able to move effectively away from pitches inside him, over his head, behind him, or occasionally even hitting him. Of course, wearing a helmet that provides good overall protection of the head should help in overcoming fear.

Hitting to all fields

The outstanding hitters of baseball are able to hit the ball to all fields. They hit the ball where it is pitched. If the ball is down the middle of the plate, they hit it up the middle. Inside pitches are pulled, and those on the outside part of the plate go to the opposite field. At all times, the good hitters are in control of the bat.

The batters who hit for average, like Rod Carew, Pete Rose, and George Brett, know how to punch the ball and push it toward left field, how to slap the ball through infield gaps, bunt for hits, and go to the opposite field. They go into the ball. That is why they are high in the averages.

Pulling the ball

In order to pull the ball, a hitter must use strong wrist action and get out in front of the ball. The bat should meet the ball before the ball reaches him. Hitting it out in front gives his swing maximum power and enables his eyes to judge the ball better. The front hip must be open and turned quickly to enable the hitter to get around.

Strong wrists, a quick eye, and fast hip rotation

are all needed to pull the inside pitch. Although some hitters find the closed stance natural for pulling, that stance sometimes leads to hip locking. Many hitters have pulling trouble because they commit themselves too quickly and pull away with the body. They find they can handle only one pitch, the inside fast ball.

A number of coaches, including Bobby Winkles, take a cautious view on pull hitting. "I have never been one to advocate pulling the ball if the player cannot do it consistently," explained Bobby. "In fact, I like to see my players hitting the ball all over the park--to all fields. I think a number of hitters have been ruined because they were told they must pull. It is either natural to pull, or it is not natural to pull. Some players can get in front and others cannot."

Hitting to the opposite field

Major league batting coaches are unanimous in declaring that the pitch on the outside corner can be handled best by hitting it to the opposite field. If the pitch is on the outside corner, the hitter should step toward the plate, pointing his toe toward right field.

To me, the best way to hit the inside pitch to the opposite field is to bring the hands in across the front of the body a little sooner, so that the big end of the bat will get on the ball. The main thing is to hit the ball squarely, If necessary, the hitter should push or punch the ball. Stepping in the direction of right field, he should keep his hands ahead of the bat and not roll his wrists. He is just slower with the bat and does not break his wrist. Contact with the ball should be made directly over the plate, not out in front. Although the batter completes a good follow-through, the weight of his body should lean toward the opposite field. If the ball is on the outside corner, the hitter should go into the pitch. If it is on the inside part of the plate, he should rotate his hip out of the way and bring in his hands and meet the ball in front of the plate.

During batting practice, I like to see a player practice hitting to the opposite field, so that he acquires the knack of moving toward the ball. When hitting to the opposite field, the hitter gives a pushing motion with his left side, and he does not let the right hand turn over. Otherwise, he will hit ground balls rather than line drives.

"In hitting the ball to the right side," said Torre, "I try to throw my hands out in front of the fat part of the bat, which causes the bat to contact the ball at an angle that directs it toward right field. When you drag the bat through, the only place you can hit the ball is to the opposite field."

The hitter has to protect the plate. If the pitcher is going to pitch outside, he has to go after that ball. He can't pull away from it and try to hit it. He has to go with it and try to hit it to the opposite field.

A right handed hitter who is able to hit the ball to right field can allow a runner at third base to score on a ground ball with less than two out.

Hitting down on the ball

Many hitters tend to uppercut slightly It is perfectly natural to swing up on a low pitch. However, if the hitter uppercuts pitches across his letters or high pitches, he will have considerable trouble. These are the pitches on which he must swing down slightly, particularly with a hard infield and if the hitter has good speed afoot. When coaches advise a hitter to come down on the pitch, generally they are referring to the letter-high pitch. By hitting down on the ball, the hitter is less likely to pop up on it.

More hitting instructors are emphasizing the slightly downward swing, the chop swing in which the hitter shortens up and swings slightly down. This type of swing will produce more line drives, rather than pop-ups into the air. To swing down on the ball, the hitter should keep his top hand on top so the wrist will not be below the front wrist at the point of contact. He should try to keep the head of the bat above the ball at all times. The reason hitters are told to swing down slightly is more or less to go to the extreme to make them level off. If a hitter levels off on a high pitch, he will hit the ball on a line.

During pepper games, hitters have the opportunity to practice hitting high pitches down. If the ball is thrown high, they can raise their arms and get the bat coming down more.

Charlie Lau method of hitting

Basically, the Lau type of hitter is one who stays off the plate, strides into the ball, attempts a level swing, and has a good weight shift. He tries to get the bat going through the strike zone in a level manner and will hit the ball where it is pitched. George Brett and Mike Schmidt both have adopted the off-the-plate, stride-into-the-ball style of hitting. By striding in, a hitter will likely keep his front shoulder in and not open up too quickly.

The three things that Lau and his hitters key on are: discipline of the head; position of the bat when the front foot hits; and weight shift. Lau strongly believes that, "If you have these three things and a little ability, you can hit!"

"The shoulder drive is very important in the hitting swing," said Lau. "You must drive your shoulder toward the pitcher. Really push it, and start pushing it out when you start your swing. The moment you fail to drive your shoulder toward the ball, your head will move and you will lose sight of the ball." The weight shift is also very important to hitting success. There has to be a transfer of weight. "A good extension of the arms will result in a good weight shift," said Lau. "As contact is made with the ball, the arms are fully extended and the head remains on the ball. The batter hits the ball when the front arm becomes straight."

Lau is a firm believer in a one-handed swing. "A dominant top hand can give a hitter problems at the point of contact," explained Lau. "When the top hand rolls or flops over, the bat head will rise a little, and as a result, he beats the ball down--smothering the ball, and it ends up a one-hopper somewhere."

In order to eliminate the problem, Lau suggested, "It helps to take the top hand off the bat after hitting the ball and try to get full extension right on through." Lau advocates releasing the top hand after driving through and making contact with the ball. This is why his hitters work so much on hitting the ball to the opposite field. They take the top hand off and get good extension with the bottom hand. This allows them to get the head of the bat out there much quicker.

"To produce a level swing, the hitter has to get on

top of the ball by swinging down on it," said Lau. "What actually happens is the bat starts down and then levels off through the swing, and at the point of contact the batter is swinging fairly level. The follow-through will be a slightly upward swing, especially if he turns loose with the top hand and lets the bottom hand get good extension." Actually, we do not believe Lau and other hitting coaches would ask their hitters to take their top hand off the bat if they could get a proper follow through. As Wait Hriniak, hitting coach of the Boston Red Sox, pointed out, "The way the hitter gets the most out of his swing is with a proper follow through. And if his hands can finish high in the swing, he will get the most out of his swing. However, some hitters have such a dominant top hand that it takes over and does not allow the bat to finish high. With this type of hitter, we ask him to release his hand after he makes contact with the ball."

Switch-hitting

Since the early 1960s, when Maury Wills popularized the practice of swinging from both sides of the plate, switch-hitting has been playing an increasing role in baseball. Certainly his ability to switch-hit changed Maury from a mediocre hitter to a good one. "I had my troubles with the curve ball," related Maury, "and I was often stepping into the bucket rather than into the ball. I was not getting enough leverage in my swing."

Switch-hitting is more suited to certain players. Coaches surveyed in a 1965 study indicated that switch-hitting requires a great amount of coordination, timing, and ambidexterity not found in the majority of people. The player ideally suited to switch-hitting is one with speed who is having definite trouble hitting one way, often a right-handed hitter. Players who have good running speed and are not blessed with great power make good prospects for switch-hitting, particularly if they are able to make good contact with the ball consistently. The chief advantage is that the switch-hitter can hit breaking stuff better. He will not be fooled by the curve ball so much. Second, as a left-hander, the player is one-and-one-half steps closer to first base.

The controlled, level swing is best for the switch-hitter. He should use a short stroke to start, With a choke grip, and should try to punch the ball. The swing should be short~ quick, flat, and even a slightly downward stroke. Ideally, switch-hitting should begin early in the player's career. Pete Rose was a ten-year-old Little Leaguer when his father taught him to swing from both sides of the plate. Wes Parker and Jim Lefebvre also switched at an early age, but Wills was an exception, inasmuch as he was twenty-seven years old when Bobby Bragan suggested the change to him in Spokane, Washington. "I think the younger a player can start the better fie will be," said Bragan.

When Wills was having considerable trouble at the plate early in the 1960 campaign, Pete Reiser, one of our coaches, took Maury under his wing and started him from scratch, almost like a manager would do with a nine-year-old Little Leaguer. "He selected a new bat for me," said Maury, "one I could whip around faster. He opened my batting stance and worked on fundamentals such as meeting the ball out in front of the plate, taking an even swing, and not overstriding."

"It boils down to practice, practice, and practice,"

said Bragan, "come out and stand on that side of the plate, and just bunt the ball. Swing easy, and see that ball coming to the plate from the other side. Hit the ball through the middle and to the opposite side of the infield. Just try to make contact and get a piece of the ball."

5

BASE RUNNING

Speed on the base paths is such a dominant factor in baseball. It can unnerve both the pitcher and the fielders. Speed also changes defensive alignments. It forces pitchers to throw more fast balls, which gives batters better pitches to hit. The combination of quick, artificial turf and the influx of new players with sprinters' speed, has significantly changed the way baseball is played and managed. Although speed is a great asset to a base runner, alertness and sliding ability are equally important. The outstanding base runner is not only quick with his feet, but is also expert at deciding when to and when not to steal. He is aggressive and full of hustle.

Speed and aggressiveness

An aggressive offense will make the defense hurry its throws and make mistakes. We have had success with good and daring base running. There are times when we have been thrown out, but speed has been important to the Dodgers' success, possibly more important than anything else.

We still believe speed will win more games than will too many slow-footed, home run hitters. If you have both, it's great, but there are not many players like Willie Mays and Mickey Mantle. Of course, the score is the big factor. When we are three or four runs behind, we do not like to take chances. However, in ordinary circumstances, when we are one run ahead or one behind and the game situation permits.

Aggressive base running pays off. It is more or less inborn, too. Some base runners are just timid and afraid. Others become lazy and then wonder why they are thrown out by one step. Baseball games can be won or lost through good or poor base running. There is nothing more frustrating for a manager than seeing his team rap out a whole flock of hits, but because of poor base running failing to score the runs they should. Then, again, there we few aspects of baseball more exciting than a hustling ball club that knows how to run the bases. The importance of good base running is obvious--more base hits, fewer double plays, more extra base hits, and many other advantages.

While aggressive base running can win ball games, being overly aggressive to the point of foolishness can also be costly. As Tim McCarver put it, "if you are going to credit speed for stealing runs, you must also discredit speed when it consistently takes you out of innings. What may have been a big inning is not."

Revival of base stealing

Base running had been a neglected art until Maury Wills arrived on the major league scene with the Dodgers in 1959. The long ball had dominated the game for years, and because of the lively ball managers were reluctant to place too much emphasis on the running game. Rather than employ such tactics as base stealing, hit and run, and bunting, they were inclined to wait for someone to hit the ball out of the park.

Except for Luis Aparicio's 56 steals in 1959, no major leaguer stole more than 40 bases in a year throughout the 1950s. Until Wills stole 104 bases in 1962, nobody in either league had stolen 70 bases in a season since Ty Cobb stole 96 in 1915. The fleet-footed Maury soon established himself as one of the great base runners in the game's history and, more than any other figure in baseball, helped bring about a return of the exciting running game. Maury made a science of getting as big a lead as possible.

Wills and Lou Brock of the St. Louis Cardinals were the premier base stealers in the 1960s. They restored base stealing to an art form. Brock, who broke Maury's record in 1974 with 118 steals, holds the major league record for career stolen bases with 938.

In 1972, Brock realized that getting as big a lead as possible was not necessarily the best approach to stealing second base. He realized that a little bit of momentum is worth much more than a little more distance. As a result, Brock developed a rolling start that provided even more impetus to the modern running game.

Brock made a science of base stealing, breaking down his leads into precise numbers of steps, calculating how long it takes a ball to go from the pitcher to catcher to second base--under optimum conditions, 2.9 seconds. Lou reacted to numerous keys and three-movement deliveries.

The three most important facets in being a top base stealer, according to Brock, are:

1. Acceleration from the start
2. Power-running

3. Acceleration within the slide

"I had two of three," said Lou. "I could run with power and had good acceleration." In 1982, Rickey Henderson of the Oakland A's shattered Brock's single-season record of 188 by stealing second base on a pitch out thrown by Doc Medich of the Milwauke Brewers. On his run for the record, Henderson stole second 88 times, third 32 times, and home plate twice. He also set another record: Most times caught trying to steal, 39. Of his total "caught stealings," 13 came from pick-off plays. Brock was thrown out 33 times in his record season.

Brock believes Rickey Henderson's shortcoming is acceleration in the slide. Lou, who is not particularly fond of the head-first slide, explained that "You're vulnerable... to spikes, knees, what-have-you. If you look at his hands, you'll see all kinds of cuts."

Although the home run is still baseball's foremost attraction, the daring, aggressive play of Wills, Brock, Henderson, and others has made major league teams more conscious of base stealing. Their success on the base paths has brought increased emphasis on base stealing and speed, providing the national pastime with added thrills and excitement.

Speed and quickness

The Dodgers have more or less insisted that the players they sign have speed. We still consider speed to be a requisite, and it always will be in this game. The game of baseball needs speed. Although we like to have some home runs too, and still believe that speed is the dominant factor, defensively as well as offensively.

When the Dodgers bring up a young player with exceptional speed, the manager is not afraid to turn him loose in a steal situation. This is because he has been through our training camp and has been instructed about getting leads and stealing bases.

Instinct and reflexes

Good instincts and reflexes are also characteristics of top base runners--to react without giving it much thought and do the right thing automatically. In deciding to take an extra base on a hit, the coach really cannot tell a player whether or not to go. If a fellow thinks he can make it, he goes ahead and runs. With other players, the manager or coach has to tell them, but there is just so much he can tell a base runner.

A ball player can be a good base runner and not necessarily have great speed. The main thing is quickness, speed of foot and quickness in deciding when to and when not to go--and getting a good break.

Mental approach

The proper mental approach is essential in becoming a successful base runner. When stealing a base, the player has to believe that he can make it. He must eliminate the fear of failing. "In stealing a base, confidence, to me, is 80 percent of the battle," said Maury, "because we know we can run, have knowledge of the pitcher and know how to get a good lead.

"A player cannot be a good base runner and practice safety first," advised Wills; "he must take chances. He should not be careless, but he has to be daring.

Knowledge of the pitcher

The runner must know the pitcher, and the moves he is going to make He should also know the catcher's arm. When taking a lead, the runner knows just how far he can go. He wants to keep the pitcher on the defensive at all times.

Even before they leave the dugout, players should watch the pitcher closely, studying his moves to the plate when he has men on base. As a player moves to the on-deck circle he should continue to watch the pitcher and study the game situation.

Game situation

The base runner is controlled by the game situation. The number of outs, the score, the ability of the base runner, who is pitching and who the hitter is at the plate, and the arms of the fielders are all factors that determine whether or not he should attempt to advance.

Running to first base

Base running begins at home plate. Batters should learn to swing so that they can recover their balance quickly in heading for first base; if the ball is hit on the ground, the concern of the batter is to cross the bag as quickly as possible

In his prime, Mickey Mantle got down to first base in 3.9 seconds batting right-handed and 3.75 to 3.8 seconds batting left-handed. If a right-handed hitter can get to first in 4.2 seconds, you can say he has good speed. The Expos have clocked Tm Raines to first in 3.57 seconds from the right side left-handed he has bee in the 3.4s.

The most important thing is to get every player to run as hard as he can as soon as he hits the ball. Ball players have to run only four or five times in a game, and yet when a ball player hits a one-hopper to the shortstop or second baseman, and it looks like an easy out, many players will not give 100 percent going down to first base. This is the first mistake the base runner makes, because anybody can kick or drop a ball; even a first baseman can drop one occasionally. To run hard from the moment he hits the ball is not asking too much of a player. In fact, that is what the fans expect, and he should do it. One of my pet peeves comes when runners do not give their very best.

The second fault of a base runner is watching the ball. Many batters keep watching the ball on a base hit. It is all right to take a quick glance at the ball to see where it is going, but once he has decided it is a base hit, the best thing to do is to go to first base as fast as possible and make his turn! Pepper Martin was one of the greatest players we have ever seen rounding first base, and he would start toward second as though he were going to make it. Then the would "slide his wheels," so to speak, and go back.

No matter what side of the plate he swings from, a batter should try to take his first step with the rear foot. As the right-handed hitter starts his swing, his body does not pull away from the plate. His stride is directly toward first base, with his rear foot, as he drops his bat with his left hand. The left-handed hitter takes a full stride with his rear foot as he drops the bat with his right hand.

The runner should go hard for first, looking only at the bag, unless the first base coach signals and yells that it is "through" and to "take your turn." The runner tries to hit first base without a jump, stepping on the center of the base as he crosses it. This is safer than hitting the front edge of the base with the toe. Some players, on the last step to first base, take a big, high jump. This should never be done. You lose time and while your foot is in the air, the ball will beat you. Even though a continuous run is best, there is no use in running far past first. The runner should slow down and listen for his base coach.

Rounding first base

When the batter sees that his hit has gone through or over the infield, he should approach first base at full speed, turning into the bag so that one of his feet hits the inside corner.

We do not like a player to take the big, wide turn at first base. Rather, the runner should head directly for first base and approximately fifteen feet from the bag, he should move three to five feet out into foul territory and prepare for a "tight, well-controlled turn." He should hit the inside part with his inside foot, but if he cannot we do not like him to break his stride. He should hit the base with either foot that comes in stride. As he hits the base from the inside, he should turn as sharply as he can and head for second and keep going until he either sees that he cannot make it or somebody stops him. Ideally, the runner should keep his body leaning toward the infield and use the inside corner of the base as a push-off point toward second base. It is also easier to hit the base with the inside foot, with the right foot then crossing over. However, we do not want a runner to break stride in order to hit the base with his inside foot.

The lead off

The base runner has to be alert when he is at first base. First, he must look and see whether the coach has a sign for him to take. He should keep one foot on the bag when he gets his signals. He should also check the positions of the outfielders, to see whether they are playing in. He must know the strength and accuracy of the catcher's throwing arm and what kind of a move the pitcher has. This is the type of knowledge that can make a player a more effective base runner.

The runner must determine how large a lead he can take and still get back to the base. He must know the pitcher, his habits and manners, and his ability to pick the runner off base. Studying the pitchers continuously, every day, is the thing that will help him steal bases.

Stance

The runner at first base should stand facing the pitcher, legs slightly bent, with his feet about a foot and a half apart. He should crouch a bit and let his arms hang loosely in front of him. His weight should be evenly distributed. He should be on the balls of his feet, so that he can go either way. Some base runners get picked off base because they are leaning toward second base. Their balance is not sufficient to make a forceful dive back to first base. The runner must keep his eyes on the pitcher at all times. He is waiting for the first indication that the pitcher will throw to the plate, and not to first base. He should not jump back and forth.

Getting the lead

Base runners, as a rule, are told to get a "good lead."

Instead, they should become proficient with time-measured leads, such as twelve, thirteen, and fourteen foot leads at first base and eighteen feet as the starting point off second.

Scouts tell me that the Expos' Raines just outruns the ball. If he gets his standard fifteen foot leadoff, Tim can steal second base in 3.3 seconds. Consider that a good pitcher takes 1.4 seconds from a stretch position to deliver the ball 60 feet, 6 inches to home plate, and a good catcher takes two seconds to receive the ball and throw it the 127 feet, 33/8 inches to second base--a time span of 3.4 seconds, not quick enough to get a speedster like Raines.

The length of the lead depends on the game situation. If it is early in the game and our runners have not seen the pitcher's moves, we tell our players: "If you are not going to steal and you want to see what kind of move he has, make him throw over there by more or less getting a good sized lead." This should be a "one-way lead." As he takes a longer lead, the player is leaning back a little toward first. Now the pitcher will throw over there a time or two, and the runner will have an opportunity to study his different moves, particularly his shoulders.

In taking his lead, the base runner should always advance his right foot first and then his left foot, keeping both feet close to the ground.

There are all types of pitchers who have really good moves to first base. Yet, when they deliver the ball, the delivery is so slow that the good base runner steals on them, in spite of a good move. While a runner cannot take much of a lead, he can still steal the base when the pitcher is delivering the ball because of the slowness of the delivery. Then, there is the other kind of pitcher who has a quick delivery but not a good move to first base. With a pitcher like this, the runner has to take a longer lead because he does not have as much time during the delivery

Returning to first base

When the pitcher steps on the rubber, the base runner should take a lead just far enough so that he will be able to get back in time to beat any throw. Some base runners will assume such a big lead that they are forced to dive or slide back to the base. Maury felt that, unless he had to dive back into first base, he did not take a good enough lead. We think this is all right for Maury, who, of course, has base running down to the fine points. When an experienced base-runner like Wills does it, he knows how far he can go and still get back safely. The college or high school boy who tries to do this, however, may get himself picked off.

The runner returns to first base by stepping back on the base with his left foot, and his body leans away from the first baseman. For most base runners, this is the proper way of returning to the bag. In leading off second base, the runner can take a longer lead. He should always listen for the base coach. In taking a lead, he should always advance his right foot first and slide his left foot, keeping both feet close to the ground. He should make sure that a ball hit to the shortstop goes through before going to third base.

One-way lead

The base runner uses the one-way lead when trying to determine the length of lead he can take on the pitcher.

He tries to make the pitcher throw to first so he can find out a little more about him. The stance is similar to the normal stance, except that most of the body weight is on the back foot (left). Therefore, the runner is "leaning" back toward the base.

Occasionally, a base runner is caught leaning. Quite likely, his balance was not sufficient to make a forceful dive back to first base. When the runner has determined how much of a lead he can take safely and is flashed the "steal" signal, then he assumes the two-way lead.

Two-way lead

With the two-way lead, the runner can go in either direction, depending on the pitcher's move. He does not take quite as long a lead as in the one-way lead. The runner must keep his weight evenly distributed on the balls of the feet and his body in a crouched position, with the knees slightly bent.

Walking lead

In this lead, the runner walks off first base casually as the pitcher is taking his set position. Lou Brock used the walking lead very effectively. Just as the pitcher indicated his intention to throw to the plate, he would break for second base, without coming to a stop--his famous rolling start. The walking lead enables base runners at first to get a good start or jump toward second base. Since the body is moving in that direction, experienced pitchers will make the runner come to a stop. This, of course, spoils the walking lead.

Getting the good jump

A good jump is the key to stealing bases. A jump is leaving for the next base the instant the pitcher commits himself to delivering the ball to the plate. A good jump is worth two-tenths of a second. Instead of taking a seventeen-foot lead and attracting numerous throws, outstanding basestealers like Rickey Henderson and Tim Raines are more comfortable taking a fourteen or fifteen foot lead, and getting a better jump. The expert base runner gets the jump on the pitcher by studying his moves and personal mannerisms. Some pitchers have all sorts of telltale things that they do. By watching him closely, the runner can spot the pitcher's peculiar little habits, which will give the runner the jump he needs. The runner should study how the pitcher lifts his foot and how he comes around with his arm. He should look for a hunch of the shoulders, a move of the elbow. Some pitchers drop their shoulder a little. Whatever he looks for, the base runner should remember to be subtle in his looking.

"One of the indications is when a pitcher stands with an open shoulder, claimed Wills. "When he is ready to throw toward home, his shoulder is usually on a line to the plate. If he wants to pick me off, he usually turns more toward first. Sometimes when a pitcher goes to first base with the ball, he stands with his feet a little closer together, or maybe the other way around. Maury likes to watch the elbow and the head. Willie Mays says he watches the pitcher's head. Others study the pitcher's feet, since the feet reveal first where the pitcher will throw.

If the pitcher commits himself with a move toward the batter, he has to throw home or a *balk is* called. As soon as the runner sees the pitcher start his pitch, he can be off and running.

Taking-off

The base runner should break for the base at the precise second the pitcher begins his move to the plate. Most runners prefer their first move toward second base to be a crossover step. When they decide to go, they just pivot on the right foot and crossover with the back foot. They should shove off for second on the left foot while pivoting on the right foot. One's weight should be forward with his legs driving hard. In shoving off for second, the runner should swing his left arm toward the next base in the same way a boxer throws an uppercut. This helps him cross over. The arm action pulls his body around and enables him to take a good first stride with his left foot.

"I always remember to keep my body moving," said Wills. "A runner can get away faster when he is in motion rather than standing still. I shuffle back and forth, bending my knees and trying to keep my weight on the balls of my feet When the pitcher starts for the plate, I start for second."

Is it easier to steal third base than to steal second base? It is easier to steal third than second because pitchers do not watch the runners on second as much as they used to. Infielders also do not bother runners like they once did.

"The only time a player should steal third base," said Wills, "is when he is positive he can make it. This is because second base is considered scoring position. To be thrown out trying to steal third base when a player is already in scoring position is a very bad play. "Of course, it is much better to be on third base than second base because there are nine more ways a player can score from third than from second."

Touching the bases

The base runner should never have to slow down to make a turn or to change strides in order to touch the bag with a certain foot. The beginning of the turn should be made from twenty to thirty feet in front of the bag.

Tagging up on a fly

The runner should have his left foot on third, with the right foot pointing toward home plate. His body should face the field, with the weight on his front foot. He goes when the outfielder catches the ball. He should not depend on the third base coach to yell, "Go!" Some players prefer a position similar to a sprinter. When on third base, the runner should tag up on any ball hit in the air, even on all foul balls.

Perhaps the fundamental least stressed and one of the most important in baseball is the art of running. While nature has endowed human beings with a basic speed, additional speed can often be obtained simply by executing the basic principles of running. A runner should keep his head up so he can see the play. Arching his neck, he leans forward without swaying or weaving. All his motion should be straight ahead. His chin should be up and his eyes on the base to which he is running. His arms should be bent at the elbow and relaxed, and the forearm should move directly forward and backward beside the body. The faster the arms are pumped, the faster the legs will move. Taking a good stride, he should run naturally on the balls of his feet.

Most good runners swing the arm forward so that the hand swings almost as high as the shoulder, and then to the rear and to the side of the hip. The right arm should go forward with the left leg, and the left arm with the right leg.

Breaking up the double play

A base runner often has the responsibility of breaking up a possible double play When sliding into second base, the purpose is not to injure the infielder but only to unbalance him and thus prevent an accurate throw to first base. Breaking up the double play, however, is illegal now in high school and college ball. Increasing efforts have been made to prevent injury at second base. Limitations have been imposed on the types of slides, rolls, blocks, etc. into second base. The runner on first base, of course, has to run hard to get to second base. Even then, on a fast double play, he does not always get there in time. In certain double play situations where the runner has time to get there, he should slide into the shortstop or second baseman, whoever is fielding the ball. While we do not want to hurt anybody intentionally, we want this runner to slide into the legs of the infielder and try to upset him. He should use a hard slide with the knees bent at a 45-degree angle, and try to hook the striding foot of the infielder.

If the shortstop should move far across the base and toward right field, the base runner should slide after him, rather than the bag. This is an accepted practice in baseball. Of course, the shortstop has the advantage. He knows whether he will cross the bag or stay in the inside, while the runner does not know. The only thing the runner can do is guess which side he will go on, and slide into him and try to knock his feet from under him.

The base runner must remember that the slide must be such that some part of the runner is within reaching distance of the bag. The runner could be charged with interference if he slides more than three feet out of the base line to hit the pivot man or if he deliberately interferes with the throw.

Use of base coaches

Whenever base runners cannot see the ball or a fielder without turning their heads very much, they should use their base coaches. They should use their own judgment as to whether or not to advance whenever they can see the ball or the fielder easily.

Runners use the first base coach for decisions on stopping at first, making the turn at first, going on to second, or hurrying back to first. They use the third base coach for stopping at second, rounding it, or going onto third, as well as directions at third base. The third base coach gets blamed for a lot of running situations over which he really does not have control. Actually, the only time he does is when a man is on first and the ball is hit down to first base and on down the right field foul line. This is when the runner has to take a quick look at the third base coach to see whether he should go or not. About twenty to thirty feet from second base, he should cut out and at the same time glance at the third base coach, then go from there. Basically, though, the runner is on his own.

Anytime the play is right in front of the runner, such as in left field, he has a better idea then someone else as to whether he can go on to third base. As long as the play is in front of him, he should be on his own.

The third base coach might walk up and say:

"Now that you are on third, we want you to go in on a ground ball," or, "Make the ball go through the infield," or, "Be sure to take off on a fly ball," and the like. Basically, though, the runner plays himself and is pretty much on his own.

Practice tips for the base runner

1. Practice getting starts on all hit balls.
2. At every opportunity, practice getting leads and starts off all bases.
3. Practice your jump in leaving first using the pivot and the cross-over push step.
4. During pre-game batting practice, practice this routine after your last swing in the batting cage: run to first, take your turn, hold up, get your lead, and break for second as the pitcher makes his pitch to the next hitter.
5. Practice taking a full swing, then follow through and try to keep from failing toward third base at the finish.
6. Practice leading off a base. Back off the bag with your rear leg behind your right. Then shuffle off to get the desired length--eight to ten feet.

Base running reminders

1. Where is the ball?
2. How many outs are there?
3. Look for a possible sign.
4. Do not talk to the opposing infielders.
5. Always run with your head up.

6. Touch all bases.
7. Watch the runner in front of you.
8. When in doubt, always slide.

A good base runner has to be able to slide, and this comes with practice. Furthermore, he must be able to slide on either his left or right side, as well as go straight in. The sooner young players learn that "it is a slide and not a leap," the sooner they will become proficient base runners. Sliding is really controlled falling. The runner simply drops to the ground according to the slide desired, and the momentum of his run does the rest.

We stress the bent-leg slide because we feel it is the most effective slide in baseball. The bent-leg slide is the safest slide for a base runner, and the top foot is going directly to the bag as quickly as it can. When a runner executes the hook slide and reaches out with his foot and tries to catch the base with his toe, he has to go an extra distance to get to the bag. When one considers that the bent leg also enables the runner to pop up and run, the value of this slide becomes apparent.

Because of the success Pete Rose, Rickey Henderson, and other big-leaguers have had with the head-first slide, more high school and college coaches are encouraging their players to use it. Both head-first and feet-first slides have strong and weak points. Therefore, other factors should be considered, such as:

1. Which slide will permit the player to get to his feet the quickest in the event of an overthrow?

2. Which slide will avoid the tag more effectively?
3. Which slide is least likely to cause injury?

Timing is essential for a good slide. The slide must not start too soon or too late, and the slider should keep relaxed when hitting the ground. As he goes into his slide, he should clench his hands loosely to avoid broken fingers. He must keep his head back and arms up. Once he decides to slide, he must go through with it. He should never change his mind! There is a proper way to fall, of course: a controlled fall, rather than a jump, which makes the slider "strawberry" prone and subject to bruises. On the bent-leg slide, most players like to take the blow all the way from the calf of their leg up to their thigh so the fall will not be concentrated on one spot.

A player has to have confidence in his ability to slide. To overcome any fear, he should practice in a sliding pit or on soft grass.

Some of the better sliders in the major leagues are capable of watching the fielder to see which side of the base he is going to field the ball on, and they will slide accordingly. During spring training, we work on this point in the sliding pits. Somebody will toss a ball each time a runner comes in, and some of the throws will be on one side of the bag and some on the other. If the slider sees that the ball is on the left side of the bag, he will slide to the right.

On several occasions, we can remember losing important runs because a player could not slide on both sides. All he had to do was slide away from the play coming into third base, but he could not, and it cost us. A player is just as good as the time he devotes to practice. Only constant practice will make a player perfect in sliding.

Bent-leg slide

The bent-leg slide is the safest slide in baseball and the most popular. Young players can become proficient quickly in this method of sliding. Along with the safety factor, it has the advantage of allowing the base runner to spring up quickly, ready to run if the ball goes through. Another advantage of the bent-leg is the fact that the~ base runner can get to the bag the quickest possible way. The bent-leg slide is the most practical one because it permits a side approach when the runner must be tagged, and a front approach on force plays. In high school baseball, where erratic throwing is more common than in professional ball, the bent-leg slide can be a great asset.

We have an occasional problem when players come down with a stiff arm to lighten their fall; they sometimes get a bruised hand or a stiff elbow. The ideal way to execute the bent-leg slide is to come in with both hands in the air. If the player can learn to take the weight of the fail on the bent leg and all the way up to the thigh, he will not get a "strawberry" or a bruise through the force of the slide.

Some players like to put dirt in their hands so that, if they slide, they do so with a closed fist. When they put their hands down, they will hit on a closed fist rather than on fingers.

The most recognized authority on the bent-leg slide is Bernie DeViveiros, former major league infielder and now a scout with the Detroit Tigers. For many years, one of DeViveiros's springtime duties with the Tigers was teaching the rudiments of the bent-leg slide to every player in the system.

The base runner should be able to slide on both sides, although it is more natural for 99 out 100 players to slide on just one leg. With the bent-leg, the side he slides on is not as important as it is with the hook slide, where he is fading away from the throw one way or the other.

The following are coaching points in learning the bent-leg slide:

1. Start to slide at least nine to ten feet from the bag. Do not slide late!
2. Take off from either leg (whichever is most natural). and bend it under.
3. Slide only on the calf of the bent leg, which must be the bottom leg.
4. Just sit down, and nature will put the correct leg under.
5. Keep low to the ground. Do not leap or jump.
6. Throw the head back as both legs bend, thus preventing the knees from hitting he ground first.
7. Turn the instep of the bottom foot so that it is facing the direction of the slide (preventing the spikes from catching in the ground).
8. Always tag with the top leg, which is raised will off the ground and is held loosely and relaxed.
9. Keep the knee slightly bent and the heel off the ground.

10. Just ride the calf of the bottom leg at all times. Use it as a wheel.

Hook slide

The hook slide is used by a runner primarily to avoid being tagged by a fielder. It can be made to either side of the base. However, we try to stay away from the hook slide, using it only in a special situation in which the runner must evade a tag. When the base runner hook slides and reaches out with that foot and tries to catch it with his toe, he is going ninety-three feet to get to the bag, rather than straight into it. Branch Rickey, whose long career included outstanding work with the St. Louis Cardinals, Brooklyn Dodgers, and Pittsburgh Pirates, called the hook slide the "93-feet slide," because the body of the base runner has gone ninety-three feet and he has not touched the base yet. This is the disadvantage of the hook slide.

The Dodgers discourage the use of the "93-foot slide," by teaching all players to extend both feet when attempting the hook slide.

When hook sliding to the right, the takeoff is usually off the left foot. Both legs are extended straight toward the base with the toes pointed, as the body falls to the right side. The right foot is slightly raised and to the right of the base. The body is almost in a flat position as the left foot and left toes touch the right corner of the base. Most of the impact is absorbed on the right hip and the right thigh.

If the runner can keep the touching foot straight as he comes in, and then it hooks, he will be all right. The key to the hook slide is to keep the touching foot straight until the runner hits the bag.

As he starts to hook slide into the bag, the runner must be sure that his catching foot, that is, the one that will touch the bag, does not bend. He must keep it pretty well straight out until he makes contact with the bag. Then, the foot stays on the bag as his body hooks on by. From the safety standpoint, the runner should be sure to get the left foot up so he does not jam it into the ground.

In sliding to his left, the runner should take off on his left foot. Both feet of the runner should be turned sideways to avoid catching the spikes in the ground. Both knees should be bent, with the weight of the upper part of the body thrown left and backward.

As he slides, the left foot should be forward and away from the base, the right leg bent and dragging, and the right foot turned so that the instep faces the base. The toes of the right foot should hook the near side of the base. While sliding, the left hand should be on the ground, palm down, to absorb some of the shock.

"Do not bend the hooking knee any more than is necessary to hook the base," said Wills. "The more the knee is bent, the longer it will take the player to touch the base."

Head-first slide

The head-first slide is being used more and more by base runners, with the idea that it is the quickest approach to the base. While few studies have been made as to which is faster, head-first or feet-first, the general feeling is that the head-first slide has the edge. The thinking is that with the head-first technique, the slider does not have to move his center of gravity back but rather moves it forward in the direction of the slide.

The head-first slide technique is not difficult to execute. Sprinting to a point ten to twelve feet from the base, the runner takes off as if diving into a pool, His arms should be fully extended, as he reaches for the base with the dominant hand. His head is slightly up as he slides along on his chest. To protect himself from injury, the slider should keep his fingers together and glide rather than bounce.

The head-first slide may be the quickest slide, but it leaves the player open to injury. However, I don't believe the head-first slide is as dangerous as it appears to be. Most of the danger is in the exposure of the hands, which can result in spike wounds. This danger may be outweighed by the fact that the Aide may be a fraction of a second faster than feet first, since the body is already leaning forward while running. Another advantage is that the eyes are always on the bag.

"The head-first slide is dangerous if you don't know what you're doing," said Frankie Crosetti. "For one thing, you are easy to tag, and the fielder can drop his knee in front of the bag and block the runner from reaching the bag.

Tips on sliding practice

A player has to have confidence in his ability to slide. To overcome any fear, he should practice in a sliding pit or on soft grass. When practicing on the grass, he should remove his spiked shoes or use tennis shoes. Sliding pads and, practice pants should be used, with long nylon or khaki shorts making good pads. In the early stages, the bases should be loose. Inexperienced sliders should start sliding at a short distance, to make sure that their legs can be bent. After the technique is mastered, the distance can be lengthened with an increase in speed. Speed is important in executing a good slide, but never forget: "You are just as good as the time you devote to practice."

Basic sliding rules

1. Once you decide to slide, go through with it. Never change your mind!
2. Make your slide with speed.
3. Remember, it is a slide and not a leap.
4. Learn to fall in a relaxed manner.
5. Concentrate on watching the base for the straight-in slide.
6. For hook sliding, concentrate mainly on the hands of the fielder.
7. On all force plays, employ a bent-leg slide.
8. Clench your hands loosely when sliding, to avoid broken fingers. Stay relaxed!
9. Any deliberate attempt on the part of a runner to spike or injure his opponent should never be tolerated.

6

BUNTING

Bunting is not a lost art in the major leagues. During the post-season playoffs and World Series in recent years, the bunting game has had a significant role in the outcome of games, as managers effectively employed the bunt to their team's advantage. The bunting game can be vital to any team's offensive strategy. An array of bunts, if used skillfully, can exert the type of pressure that can have an unsettling effect on the defense, particularly when the bunts are executed with surprise and deception. When a runner has to be advanced, the batter must be proficient in executing the sacrifice bunt. True, the great urge to go for the long ball, emphasis on base stealing, and the running game have resulted in less bunting on the major league level. There is more speed on the bases, people who can "fly," and some managers are reluctant to give up an out. Artificial playing surfaces, of course, have cut down on bunting, because many bunters bunt the ball too hard. Additionally, today's defensive alignments are more effective in defending against the bunt, especially on astroturf.

Bunting can and should be a valuable offensive weapon, even for sluggers like Gary Carter and Steve Garvey. "I believe bunting is a very important part of my game," said Carter. "Every player should be able to bunt effectively." Garvey, with an occasional bunt, has made the defense come to him. He does not allow the third baseman to play back forty-five feet and take away his base hits. The threat of the bunt tends to keep the defense honest. To stay out of the double play, the offensive team has to use the bunt to advance runners and provide the opportunity for them to score on a base hit. "I think it is important for all hitters up and down the lineup to be capable of bunting," said Steve Boros, manager of the Oakland A's. "This doesn't mean a team should bunt that much, but when it has the capability, there is always fear in the opposition's mind."

There are a number of reasons for the shortage of good bunters today. Perhaps the biggest one is the great urge on the part of teams to go for the long ball. The more power a team has, the less likely it will bunt. Many players, in fact, do not want to bunt. They would rather hit. As a result, they do not devote the time and practice to develop bunting skill.

Laying the ball down can be a difficult assignment, particularly if the pitcher keeps the ball high. Bunt defense has improved considerably. With the first and third basemen drawn way in, the sacrifice can be a tough play to perform. The first baseman is charging in. On our club, for instance, we had two or three set bunt defenses. Using signs, we would go from one to the other, and we did one thing on one pitch and another thing on another pitch. The bunt defense has improved to such a degree that the offense really has to have its bunting game down.

Furthermore, young ball players today just do not practice as much as people did in the past. "Years ago, a guy would go out and practice for a half-hour a couple times a week," said Jim Frey, Major League manager and coach. "Now, you are lucky if they will practice twenty minutes a season."

"Bunting is a lost art it you don't work on it," said Joe Garagiola. Well, bunting need not be the "lost art" if the coach and squad are willing to spend time and use the proper techniques in bunting. Through the years, numerous college and high school coaches have won many games on a sacrifice bunt or a suicide squeeze. Yet, these coaches did not have good bunters--they developed them by practicing the proper techniques.

Every player should not only learn how to bunt, but should devote part of his daily hitting practice to laying down bunts. While the sacrifice bunt has to cope with superlative defenses at the major league level, the bunt can produce huge dividends at lower levels of play. Many supposedly poised defenses have been completely demoralized by a variety of safe bunts in a row. When one considers how often bunts can get a team started--get the first man on base--it is quite easy to respect the little bunt as a major weapon.

Good technique

The bunting game, in general, is not as good as it used to be. Perhaps the major reason for faulty bunting techniques is poor position. Many young players are so interested in reaching base safely and getting a base hit that they neglect to bunt properly. In their haste to get a good start to first base, many bunters are not squared around in time. Consequently, bunters try to bunt the ball behind the plate instead of out in front of the plate. In addition, they start for first base too quickly, before the bunt is made. If they would square around, get set, and make the ball come to the bat, they would be on their way to becoming proficient bunters. Good bunters hold their bat fairly high, at the height of the strike zone. Pitchers are instructed to throw the ball high because the high pitch is the toughest ball to bunt. To combat this, the bunter should hold his bat at the top of the strike zone. This will enable him to go down rather than up, on any pitch in the strike zone. It is easier and quicker to bring the bat down than to raise it.

There arc several theories as the actual technique of laying the ball down properly. Some coaches teach their players to hold the bat in their fingers, so that when the ball meets the bat it just hits the bat back into their hands. This technique tends to deaden the ball enough. Another theory is that the bunter has to "give" slightly with the bat when the ball makes contact. The idea is to make the ball come to the bat and "catch the ball" on the bat.

Bunting stances

Basically, there are two bunting positions: the square-around and the pivot-in-tracks. For many years, bunters have squared around with the entire body, pulling the front foot back and toward the outside of the box. However, many players today do not square around to face the pitcher. Rather, they keep their feet planted and pivot in their tracks. They square only their hips and shoulders to bunt. Which style is more effective and easier to execute, is an individual thing. The position that best suits the player should be used. The idea behind a batter pivoting on the balls of the feet to bunt is to prevent the defense from knowing as long as possible he is going to bunt.

Square-around

The square-around stance places the bunter in a better position to handle the ball. When he squares around, the bunter has a little better coverage of the entire plate. When bunters use the pivot-in-tracks method, they sometimes fail to get the bat out far enough in front, and it is sometimes a little hard to reach the outside of the plate.

To execute the square-around, the right-handed bunter pulls the left foot back and toward the outside of the box. The right foot is then moved forward slightly to put the shoulders of the bunter perpendicular to the pitcher. The feet of the bunter are about shoulder width apart and parallel to each other. The inside foot is placed on the inside line of the box, as close to the plate as is legal. By flexing the legs in a squat or by leaning slightly outward, the bunter can cover the entire strike zone. Increasingly, bunters are squaring away earlier, with the philosophy: "Who cares if I tip the play? The sacrifice is no surprise anyway" The fielders will be charging in on the grass. The batter should move into bunting position as soon as the pitcher lifts his striding foot and leg. By squaring early, the bunter may get infielders charging too much, then he can chop it past them.

Pivot-in-tracks

Many team no longer want players to square-around and face the pitcher when they sacrifice. The majority of big-league players square only their hips and shoulders and keep their feet planted to bunt. The important point is to get the bat out in front of the plate in a position to reach even the outside pitch. Many bunters simply twist their feet at the last instant, and they find themselves off balance for the outside strikes. The bunter remains in his tracks and on the balls of his feet. He merely pivots his feet toward the pitcher. He pivots on the heel of the front foot, so that the toe is pointing toward the pitcher, and on the ball of the back foot just enough to turn the foot a little. This turns the shoulders and hips so he is facing the pitcher.

"I prefer to keep the feet in the hitting position and just turn the upper part of the body toward the plate," said infielder Phil Garner. "This is the technique I feet most comfortable with, but a player should do what he does best, whatever it takes to get the ball down. Sometimes, form is not an essence when you are trying to get the job done."

Actually, the bat position for the pivot-in-tracks is the same as for the square-around position. The bunter can swing his hips around and square them to the pitcher without lifting his feet off the ground. By using the pivot-in-tracks method, the bunter will help keep the infielders from charging too quickly. "Many times, instead of squaring around, I will turn the upper half of my body without stepping at all," said Mark Belanger, one of baseball's premier bunters. "What it does is not give the bunt away so quickly, which in turn enables the batter to make it more of a surprise.

Bunting technique

Body position

The bunter's body should be in a slight crouch and leaning toward the plate, to make sure the plate is well covered. The trunk and knees are slightly bent and most of the body weight is placed on the front foot.

Being up in the front part of the batter's box gives the bunter a better opportunity to bunt the ball fair. His knees should be slightly bent and flexible. The weight should be on the balls of the feet, slightly forward. "A bunter has to keep his legs relaxed," said infielder Craig Reynolds, another excellent bunter. "He can't bunt stiff-legged. On a low pitch, he has to bend his knees. He can't reach and jab at the ball. He must bend down at the knees on a low pitch."

Arms and hands The arms should be relaxed, out in front of the bunter's body. The bat should be held parallel to the ground chest-high and covering the plate, with the elbows near the body The right hand should slide up close to the trademark as the bat is leveled off. The bat should be gripped lightly with the upper hand, keeping the fingers underneath and the thumb on top. The thumb and index finger form a "V".

"Keep the hands away from the body," advised Belanger. "If they are tied up inside and the bat is kept close to the body, the bunter has a tendency to stab at the ball. Keep the bat head above the hand. Let the ball hit the bat and kind of give with the ball. Don't stab at it or push the ball. You want to deaden the ball, so allow the ball to hit the bat." The barrel end of the bat is extended in front of the body and points toward, the pitcher. The hands and arms should give as the ball is met, as if the bat were catching the ball. Cup the bat with the top hand without curling the fingers around it. The grip on the bat should be mainly with the thumb, index finger, and middle finger. The other fingers should be tucked in and under the bat. The more firmly his hands grip the bat, the harder the batter will bunt the ball.

"A bunter should grip the bat more or less in his thumb and forefinger, with a real light touch," said Frey. "Some people say, 'You should catch the ball with the bat,' but I don't know if that is exactly correct. You should not squeeze the bat and jab at the ball. Hold the bat loosely so that when the ball hits the bat, it is not a real solid contact. A bunter should try to deaden the ball. He doesn't want to push the ball out there. The only instance where a bunter wants to push the ball is when he is pushing the ball past the pitcher on the first base side." Caution must be taken not to wrap the index and middle fingers around the bat, which would allow the ball to hit them. The loose hand near the end of the bat makes it easier to angle the bat, and helps produce a soft bunt.

Eyes The bunter's eyes should be on the ball. From the start of the pitcher's delivery to the actual contact of the ball on the bat, the eyes should be focused on the moving ball. Only good balls, those in the strike zone, should be bunted. Successful bunting, like hitting, requires not only good eyesight, but knowledge of the strike zone.

Bat position There are two schools of thought on the position of the bat. Many bunting instructors like to keep the bat level--parallel to the plane of the ground--at all times. Others teach their bunters to keep the bat diagonal, to keep the point of the bat in the air.

Jim Frey believes the bat should be on a diagonal to the ground, at a 45-degree angle. "The barrel of the bat should be kept above the hands," said Frey. "To keep the ball out of the air, a bunter should keep his bat on top of the strike zone and then drop the barrel of the bat on the ball down in the strike zone. The back hand has to be higher than the front hand. If the pitch is above the strike zone, he should take it." The barrel of the bat should be above the hands, and when the bunter actually makes contact with the ball and the bat gives with it, the bat will automatically be level. Whether it starts out level or not, upon contact with the ball, the bat should be level, as shown in Figure 2.3. In the third picture, Belanger brings his bat back to deaden the ball. Once he determines whether he is bunting toward third or first, the bunter must set the angle of his bat immediately. As the ball approaches the bunting area, he adjusts the angle of the bat. If he is going down the third base line, the barrel is pointed right at first base.

A bunter then must get the bat out in front of him. Many players end up with the bat behind them, which creates many foul balls. "If you are bunting left-handed, you would want the left hand or the back hand out in front where you can see the ball hit the bat," explained Frey. "Try to bunt the ball toward the end of the bat, which will deaden the ball."

"Getting the bat out in front of the plate is the biggest problem in bunting," emphasized Boros. "Some players are a little reluctant to get close to the plate. In order to be a good bunter, the bunter has to almost get his nose in it and get the bat out in front of the plate." When the ball makes contact with the bat and hits the ground, it has a much better chance of staying fair if the bat is out in front of the plate," said Belanger. "Whereas if the bat is back, sometimes the ball will hit the plate and bounce foul."

Mental stance

"Staying relaxed when bunting is very important," said

Billy DeMars, veteran big-league coach. "Quite often, as soon as the hitter looks down and sees that it is the bunt sign, he has a tendency to get a little nervous or upset, and this places pressure on him. He must stay relaxed, loose, and stay back on the rear leg." Fear of the ball is a major reason for faulty bunting technique, according to Coach Dave Bristol. "Many young players are afraid of the ball," said Dave. "They want to make sure the ball doesn't hit them, and then they say, 'I will try to bunt it then.' You can't be afraid of the ball!"

When bunting, a player must first get a good pitch to bunt. Many hitters can be very patient when swinging, but when they are bunting for a base hit, they are so anxious to get a good break out of the box, that they bunt at a lot of bad balls.

Types of bunts

There are two kinds of bunts the sacrifice bunt and 2) bunting for a base hit--the drag and the push bunts.

Sacrifice bunt

With runners on first, or first and second, the bunt is still considered good baseball by the great majority of managers and coaches, particularly with no outs. First, the runners can be advanced into scoring position, and, second, the double play threat is eliminated. "In executing the sacrifice, the bunter has to concentrate in his mind what he wants to do before the play occurs," said Garner. "He must get himself in the bunting position soon enough, not wait until the pitch is already on the way. True, the big-leaguers are capable of waiting until the last second, just dropping the bat down." Bunters often try to bunt the ball too perfectly down the line. They end up having the ball roll foul. If the ball is bunted properly and not too hard, and if it is halfway between the pitcher and catcher, it is a pretty sure bunt. The key rule in executing the sacrifice bunt is for the hitter to give himself up. The purpose of the sacrifice bunt is to advance the runner at the expense of the bunter. The bunter is expendable! Making a good bunt is the main objective. The placement of sacrifice bunts depends on which bases are occupied, the defensive positions of the opposition, and the opposition's ability to field bunts. Normally, a sacrifice bunt should not be used unless the runner or runners, when advanced, could tie the score or put the offensive team ahead.

On a straight sacrifice bunt, the batter attempts to bunt the ball only if the pitch is a strike. He must realize that he should bunt only good balls that are in the strike zone, unless, of course, the suicide squeeze play is on. With first base occupied, a bunt down the first base line is considered good baseball. The first baseman, holding the runner on first base, will not be in a good position to field the ball, since he does not leave the base until the pitcher delivers. With second base occupied, a hard bunt down the third base line can be a good tactic. When the third baseman comes in to field the ball, he leaves third base uncovered.

Run-and-bunt play This play is a variation of the sacrifice bunt, in which the base runner attempts a steal of the next base. To protect the runner, the hitter must bunt the ball regardless of where it is pitched. A good time to execute this play is when the pitcher is behind in the count and therefore more likely to make the next pitch a strike. The best game situation is with none out and a runner on first base.

Bunting for a hit

To surprise the defense and make a safe hit, the batter might attempt to beat out a bunt. The bunt base hit is a beautiful thing to watch because it takes great skill, and plenty of action is involved. This bunt technique is used when the third baseman is playing deep. The bunter steps one stride backward with his right foot to the left of the plate, as the weight shifts to the left foot. Once the feet are set, the weight should be shifted again to the right foot. The head of the bat points toward first base. The ball can either be pushed toward first base (right-handed bunter) or dropped down the third base line. The batter conceals his intent until the last split-second and meets the ball on the move.

If the pitcher uses slow pitches and curves, it is easier to bunt the ball on the ground than it is if he uses fast balls. There is always danger in base hit bunts, in that once the hitter has decided to use it, he has a tendency to bunt the ball even if it is not where he wants it. He must learn to snap the bat back out of the way of bad pitches. The left-handed batter has an advantage over a right-hander in bunting for a base hit, since he is more than a full step nearer first base. The left-handed swinger who is quick on his feet and a skillful bunter can be a real threat to the defense, particularly on a drag toward the second baseman.

Push bunt (right-handed batter) This offensive tactic is used when the first baseman is playing deep. The push bunt is directed toward the pitcher's left, the first base side of the infield. The batter stands at the plate, decoying a possible swing at the ball. As the pitcher cocks his arm in his delivery, the batter rotates his hips to the rear as if he wanted to take a full swing.

"I will tell the player to hide the play as long as possible," said Boros, "and not to drop the bat into the bunting area until the pitcher's arm starts to come forward. This gives the hitter time enough to get the bat out in front of the plate and yet disguise the play from the defensive player." "I like to see a right-hand hitter drop his right foot back," said Boros. "If the pitch is inside, he can step back a little and have a little bunting room inside. If the pitch is outside, then the hitter simply leans forward and pushes the ball down between the first baseman and the pitcher."

Aiming for the hole between first and second base, the batter takes a short lead step with his front foot as the bat is pushed at an outside pitch. He must meet the ball before his right foot hits the ground. The ball is pushed or pulled by manipulating the near hand on the bat handle, sending the ball in the desired direction. This type of bunt must be hard enough to get by the pitcher. It should be used only when the first baseman is playing back.

Pushing the ball past the pitcher on the first base side can be very effective. The idea is to make the first baseman go to his right and to allow the batter to beat the pitcher to the bag. Or, if a left-handed pitcher has a tendency to fall off toward the third base side, a hitter can bunt the ball to the right side of the mound making the first baseman and second baseman field the ball. The bunter then has a good chance to beat the pitcher to the bag. In this instance, the bunter should push the ball hard.

Push bunt (left-handed batter) A left-handed hitter just wants to touch the ball. He does not want to bunt the ball as hard as does the right-handed bunter. The left-handed bunter wants the ball to die about twelve to fifteen feet down the third base line. We try to tell the young left-handed bunters to bunt the ball out toward the end of the bat, where the ball will die naturally. The crucial thing with left-handed bunters is to get them to take their first step at the pitcher so they do not pull away from the pitch too soon. Many players who try to bunt the ball down the third base line want to run to first base too quickly. "You have to wait and bunt the ball and make a good bunt, then you run," said Bristol.

Drag bunt (left-handed batter) The drag bunt is one of baseball's most exciting and potentially explosive plays. However, it is a play that requires concentration, timing, and practice. The drag bunt can be a valuable offensive weapon for a left-handed batter, usually when the first baseman plays deep. The objective is to bunt the ball to the left of the pitcher, and hard enough so that the pitcher cannot field the ball, forcing the first baseman or second baseman to do so. Success in the drag bunt comes only when the defense is not expecting the play.

Any player with outstanding speed who has little power should perfect the drag or push bunt which will keep the infield close. With the fast playing surfaces of today, the little player with speed will find it easier to be successful. But success requires practice and the great determination that Maury Wills and other smaller players have demonstrated through the years.

The batter stands at the plate decoying a possible swing. As the pitcher cocks his arm in his delivery motion, the batter may rotate his hips to the rear as though meaning to take a full swing. This is a perfect example of how the drag bunt should be executed. He sets the angle of the bat so that the big end points halfway between third base and home plate. The bat is approximately at a right angle with the side of his body. His right hand holds the bat at the end, and his left hand is on the trademark. Maury's bat contacts the ball out in front of the plate. Notice the perfectly level bat at contact with the ball. When contact is made, his weight is on his right foot, and his left foot trails slightly, ready to cross over the right leg.

The biggest fault of players on the drag bunt is crossing over too quickly with the left foot, since most left-handed bunters run away from the ball. They try to run before they really make contact, because they are more intent on getting a good start than on bunting the ball. It is like catching a ball: the fielder has to catch it before he throws it. Likewise, in bunting, the ball has to be bunted before the play can be made. In executing a drag bunt correctly, the bunter should step toward the ball with his right foot and meet the ball before his left foot hits the ground. Some bunters prefer to take a short step with the right foot, and then step over with the left.

Fake bunt

In a bunt situation, when the infield is in too far for safe bunting, the batter may want to fake a bunt and swing or slap at the ball. This is also effective when a runner is trying to steal a base. This bothers the catcher not only in receiving, but in throwing the ball as well.

In still another situation, the hitter may assume a bunting position in the hope that the first and third basemen will charge in toward the plate. If the infielders charge, the batter will move both hands up on the handle of the bat and chop down hard on the pitch. He tries to bounce the ball through or over the charging fielders. The batter should square around to bunt or pivot in his tracks, and then fake a bunt. His hands should be together but fairly high on the bat. As the pitcher releases the ball, the hitter should rotate his hips slightly toward the catcher and take a short swing, stepping with his front foot toward the ball as he swings.

If the runner on third is stealing home, the hitter may fake a bunt and hold his ground. It will help the runner and make it harder for the catcher to tag him, especially if the hitter is right-handed. The batter can also use the fake bunt when taking a pitch or a strike. He should make his move before the pitcher releases the ball to distract the pitcher and make it harder for him to get the ball over the plate.

Squeeze play

The purpose of the squeeze play is to bring a man home from third base. The prime objective of the blunter is to meet the ball and to get it on the ground. Usually the squeeze is employed to tie the score, score the winning run, or provide an insurance run for the team that is ahead.

Safety and suicide plays are usually tried in the late innings with a runner on third base, one out, and the team at bat ahead, tied, or no more than one run behind.

Safety squeeze The batter bunts the first good ball he gets--he bunts only strikes. The runner does not run for home until he sees that the ball is bunted.

The runner at third base should make his move only if the ball is bunted on the ground. As soon as the pitcher releases the ball, he is ready to run. If the ball is popped up or missed, the runner does not go. The batter should try to bunt the ball away from the pitcher. If the first baseman is back, the bunter's objective is merely to tap the ball down the first base line.

Suicide squeeze The bunter must bunt the ball regardless of where it is thrown. He must try just to bunt the ball in fair territory and on the ground. The runner at third base knows the batter will bunt the next pitch, no matter where it is, so he starts for home the moment the ball leaves the pitcher's hand. He must make his move at the right time. The play will be in trouble if the runner is late breaking or is too early. The bunter must protect the runner from suicide by making sure to bunt the ball on the ground in fair territory.

"In a squeeze situation, a major problem is that many players try to make too careful of a bunt," said Frey. "They try to place the ball too much. In a squeeze situation, the batter has to bunt the ball out in front of the plate--get the ball down and the runner is going to score. But there are many foul balls on suicide squeeze plays, and the biggest reason is that the bunters are trying to make too good of a placement."

The only way a ball player can become a better bunter is to practice. Dave Bristol likes to see players go out and play pepper every day and work on their bat control. Pete Rose plays pepper every day, and, often, about every fourth or fifth ball, he will just bunt the ball either to first or third base. Just the fact that he keeps doing it, the repetition, and doing it properly is what makes Pete an outstanding bunter and the great hitter he is.

As Mark Belanger pointed out: "A player can't go out there after a month of no bunting practice and expect to bunt the ball effectively. Bunting is a very difficult thing to do and requires continual practice."

7

TEAM OFFENSE

Types of offense

The type of offense used depends entirely on the type of *club* the manager or coach has, whether it is a power or a speed *club.* The type of pitching that he has is another determining factor.

The manager or coach often tries to estimate how many runs his opponent is going to get. If someone like Koufax is pitching, I will say: "OK, let's bunt in the first inning, or steal the base, try to get one run, and hope that we can hold it."

A team that lacks the home run hitters should have players who are able to bunt, drag, and push, and have all sorts of ways to bring the infield in. With the infield in, the offense has a better chance to hit the ball past the infielders for a base hit.

The home run is a great weapon. But if the manager does not have this type of hitter, he has to go the other way. In fact, good pitching generally can handle good home run hitters because they are free-swingers. They either hit the ball out of the park, or they hit into a double play, or strike out. With the infield back, they are not as much of a threat as is the hitter who slaps the ball around and can bunt, drag, and run.

Hitting away is not the only way to score, runs. Bunting, the steal, hit-and run, run-and-hit, and the squeeze play can all advance runners to scoring position of score them. In a close game, when one run can mean victory, the advancement of a base runner can be a significant factor in the outcome. The ability to move runners along is a requisite for a winning ball team. With a runner on second and nobody out, the hitter has to get him to third. If he can't hit behind the runner, fie has to bunt him over. With a runner on third base and less than two outs, the batter must get him home. To be a winner, a team must do this very well.

Emphasis on power and speed

Major league clubs today, are emphasizing power and speed. "If a team has power and good hitters, it will hit away," explained Steve Boros. "If a team has speed, it will run with them—either steal or hit-and-run. Unless we get late in the ball game, we really don't utilize the bunt that much. In the American League with the designated hitters, teams are going more and more to either the running or the hitting game in a bunt situation. Many coaches and managers today refuse to give that out, and they prefer moving the runners around some other way."

An aggressive offense

Basically, the more aggressive a team can be, the more successful it will be. This starts with the hitter himself. The hitter has to be aggressive and believe that every pitch is going to be a strike. He should start after every pitch and be able to hold back if the pitch is a ball. Then, he must run hard from the moment he hits the ball until he rounds first base or second and is stopped by the play. His own judgment may force him to stop, or the coach may hold him up. As soon as he is on first base, the base runner immediately has to "think positive" that he might be able to steal second. When he gets the sign, he must be ready with his lead and break quickly with the proper cross-over step. If the hitter gets a hit behind him, he should not be satisfied in stopping at second; but should go to third or as far as he can go within reason. *He must be aggressive all the way.*

The offense must exert continual pressure on the defense, and in doing so, they force mistakes. When a top base stealing threat such as Rickey Henderson gets on first base, he can exert considerable pressure on the pitcher. The pitcher will say to himself: "I've got to throw over there three or four times. I've got to rush my delivery." He becomes so concerned about the man on first stealing second that he gets behind the hitter. In addition, this concern takes a little concentration away from the pitcher, which is very helpful.

When the base runner gets on first base, the outfielders are thinking: "With this man on first, the chances are that he will be going to third. An aggressive hitter goes after the ball. He really wants to go after it, and, if it is in the strike zone, he will swing at it. If it is not in the strike zone, it is like seeing the red light on the street. Everything is green and his foot is on the gas until he sees the red light. Then he has to stop. With practice, this becomes a réflex action, but the most important attributes of an aggressive hitter is that he starts after every pitch and really wants to hit it. This is the attitude a hitter should have.

Pressure on the defense

An effective running game, sparked by well-executed bunts, the steal, and hit-and-run, and highlighted occasionally by the exciting squeeze play, can place considerable pressure on defense. The drag bunt, clever and daring base running and skilful sliding are methods and techniques that develop the fast-moving situations that cause mechanical and mental errors by the defense. Indeed, an aggressive offense has many advantages over the team which plays conservative, safe baseball. The threat of a steal will often cause pitchers to lose their concentration on the hitter, while the threat of a bunt will bring in the infield, decreasing their fielding coverage. Thus, the element of threats can be effective in keeping the defense off-balance and unsettled.

There is nothing nicer to see than a player getting a base hit and rounding the base at full speed. When he decides to stop, he almost slides his wheels and goes back. If he rounds the base properly and the outfielder just juggles the ball, he may keep going right into second base. These are the things that can get that one or two extra runs a team needs to win.

True, there are times when the runner is thrown out. It looks bad in these instances but, percentagewise over the season, this aggressive style of play pays off. Certainly, the coach finds it easier to slow his runners down and make them a little more cautious than to make them more aggressive.

An early lead

One of the pleasant aspects of baseball is that, if a team can get out in front early in the game, the coach can do so many things. He can hit-and-run, steal, or sacrifice if he is a run or two in front. But as soon as he gets behind three or four runs, he cannot do so many things. He can neither take wild chances nor can he keep the pressure on the defense. So, he has to sit around and wait until his team collects three or four hits in a row.

Importance of speed

Speed is as extremely valuable offensively, as it is defensively. To win today, a baseball team has to run the bases, take good leads, and go from first to third. The player with speed has a greater advantage in beating out the infield hit. He will go from first to third on 90 percent of the base hits, more so than the slow-footed fellow who has to stop at second. The runner at second base with good speed is difficult to throw out at home plate.

Some of baseball's best teams have achieved success largely on exceptional speed. The Dodgers have played, and still play, for one run, using the hit-and-run, the steal# and the bunting game. The runner at second may steal third and score on an infield ground ball. Actually, a team may go this route the entire game and be able to pick up three or four runs from these tactics. However, it has to be a team that has speed, can bunt, and is able to move the ball around, such as with the hit-and-run play arid hitting to the opposite field.

Whitey Herzog, who was largely responsible for developing the 1969 Mets, the Kansas City Royals, and the St. Louis Cardinals, has never placed emphasis on power. He is always looking for speed. "I don't mind having some power hitters who can play defense," explained Whitey.

"With a speed team like the Cardinals," said Herzog, "if we're down two runs going into the eighth, we still may try to steal. That way if we get the steal, we would score on a single and stay out of a double play. Every time you steal a base, you generally only need one hit to score a run," said Herzog. "If you don't steal, you need two hits. I think it's easier to steal a base than it is to get two hits."

Team lineups today are sprinkled with swift runners who can steal and take the extra base on a hit. Speed can unnerve both the pitcher and the fielders. Speed also changes defensive alignments. By forcing pitchers to throw more fast balls, it gives batters better pitches to hit.

Aggressive attitude

Building an aggressive attitude, offensively and defensively, should be the prime concern of the coach or manager. An aggressive offense is particularly demoralizing to a high school team. Quite frequently, the team that scores first breaks the opponent's spirit. A high school team cannot rely consistently on the hitting prowess of their top hitters in a scoring situation. Instead, the coach must develop techniques and plays, such as the steal, to compensate for his team's uncertain hitting and to support scoring potential.

The aggressive, positive type of coach who takes the initiative and employs the elements of surprise and deception in his offense can achieve considerable advantage.

Batting order

The forming of a batting order is not as simple as it

seems. The manager or coach must arrange his batting order according to the players he has available. He should try to balance his lineup so that the attack is as strong as possible from the lead-off man through the ninth hitter. The lead-of man should have a good "on base" average; he should be a fairly good hitter, although not necessarily a long ball hitter. He is the type of hitter who has a good eye and does not swing at bad balls. Possessing good speed, he should have two or three ways to get on base.

The lead-off man must get on base. The 1982 world champions St. Louis Cardinals has a very revealing statistic. When their lead-off man walked, he scored 42 percent of the. Any manager will settle for almost half a run for every time get the lead-off man on.

The number two man should have the bat control to hit-and-run and go behind the runner. He must be a man who can lay the ball down if the sacrifice is needed. He should be able to pull the ball if he has to, or go the other way when the occasion calls for it. Some managers feel there is an advantage in having a left-handed swinger in the number two spot. If he is a left-handed hitter, he can hit the ball through the hole. The right-handed swinger should be encouraged to go to right field.

Generally, the number three man is faster than the number four hitter. I like to have my speed Lip in front. The number four hitter would be the RBI man who has the most power. He should be the hitter who occasionally can hit one out of the park. There is not a great deal of difference between the four and five hitters. The number six man is the next power hitter, although not as good as the three, four, or five men. The seventh, eighth, and ninth positions are filled with the three weakest hitters playing. As a rule, the pitcher will bat in the ninth position, but the catcher is not always necessarily the eighth man in the lineup. In high school ′ and sometimes in college play, the pitcher may be one of the better hitters on the team.

Offense tactics

Hit-and-run

The hit-and-run is one of the greatest plays in baseball, but it requires a hitter with good bat control to hit the ball through the hole. He should be told to hit the ball on the ground. If he cannot get a piece of the ball, the runner will likely be thrown out by the catcher. This is because, on the hit-and-run, the base runner does not get the daring lead that he would if he were stealing.

There have been some fine right-handed hitters who could go to the opposite field and had the bat control to go to the spot the fielder was leaving. If the coach does not have this type of hitter at the plate, he should tell the batter to just be sure to get a piece of the ball and hit it on the ground. If he hits it in the air, everything is lost. While the runner at first can be bunted over, the right type of hitter can accomplish more by hitting the ball into right field, thereby ending up with men on first and third. Besides, defences against the bunt have become so formidable that many big-league managers are employing the hit-and-run more than they did in the past.

The purpose of the hit-and-run play is to advance the runner an extra base and to protect him from the double play. It is often used in the middle or late stages of the game. It is a good play when the pitcher is behind the batter, especially on the three-and-one pitch. With a runner on first base, the right-handed hitter will often try to hit the ball behind the runner, thinking the second baseman will cover. The batter must swing at the ball wherever it is pitched, even if he has to throw the bat at it. "Executing the hit-and-run takes a certain knack on the part of the hitter," said Bobby Hofman. "You must work on it. You have to wait until the ball gets to the plate. Bill Rigney taught me just to keep my right elbow into my side so I cannot get the bat out in front of my body. You lead with your hands. The hands are out in front and you just try to hit the ball to right field."

If the catcher guesses and calls for a pitchout, the offense, of course, is in trouble,. If a wild pitcher is on the mound, a manager is a little reluctant to put the hit-and-run on.

Run-and-hit

Instead of hitting behind the runner, the hitter simply tries to hit the ball, which for young, inexperienced players, is an easier skill to execute. The runandhit can cause many problems for the defense, such as breaking up a double play with a slow runner at first. A good time to call for a runandhit is when the pitcher is behind in the count, because he must come in with the pitch. The runner should be on the move, and the hitter is instructed to go for the ball if it is in the strike zone. The runandhit is used more with a fast runner on base. If the pitch isout of the strike zone, the runner has a chance to steal a base.

The hitter should know that the runner is going, and if it is in the strike zone, "I am going to be cutting." The worst thing that can happen on a runandhit is for the runner to go and then have the hitter take the pitch right down the middle.

Hitting behind the runner

When the situation is right, some managers prefer hitting behind the runner rather than employing the bunt or a hit-and-run play. This offensive tactic is usually attempted when only first base is occupied and there are less than two out. In an effort to advance the runner on first to second base, the hitter tries to hit the ball on the ground between the first and second baseman. The runner will break for second. Many times, there is a lot of space in there to hit the ball behind the runner. The batter should attempt just to meet the ball. Right-handed hitters find it effective to go after an outside pitch. With a man on second base, the manager will usually try to advance him to third base. With the bunt play proving not as successful as it used to be, many teams will have the batter go to the opposite field. The batter should try to hit the ball on the ground.

Hit the ball to the opposite field

The batter who has the short, quick stroke and quick wrists is the fellow who is likely to have the bat control necessary to hit the ball consistently to the opposite field. Whether this is hand-and-eye coordination or what, some hitters have it and some do not. The double play is a, great morale booster for the defensive team. That is why I want my players to find a way to hit the ball to the opposite field. By doing so, the batter is hitting away from the double play, and, more important, we have runners on first and third with only one out.

Getting a run with an out

One of baseball's unsung heroes is the hitter who is capable of getting a run with an out. With a man on first or second base, he can hit the ball consistently to right field, moving the runner around. When that one run is so important, the hitter should actually sacrifice himself in order to score the run. All he has to do is hit the ball on the ground,

Therefore, a hitter should know how to make himself be put out. He must be able to ground the ball to the second baseman, especially when the infield is not in. He has to concentrate all the time to "Get the Fun! Get the run!'

If the first man doubles, the next man should ground the ball to second base, moving the runner to third. If a left-handed hitter comes up with a man on first base, he should not even dare to think of hitting the ball to left field. For two reasons, he has to think about driving the ball through that hole. If he singles to right field, we are *on* first and third. If he singles to left field, we are on first and second, and still in jeopardy. But, if we have a man on third base, then *they* are in jeopardy because, now, we can get a run with an out.

Run-and-bunt play

This play is a variation of the sacrifice bunt, in which the base runner attempts a steal of the next base. To protect the runner, the hitter must bunt the ball regardless of where it is pitched. On occasion, the run-and-bunt play is used more or less as a surprise tactic. With the bunt in order, the first baseman charges in, and as he moves in quickly it is difficult for him to know whether or not the runner has left. Under ordinary circumstances, he will make the force play at second, but the man at first is already running and often beats the throw. This play can be dangerous, however. If the hitter pops the ball up, misses it completely, or it is a bad pitch, the runner might get thrown out. We feel it is a good play, though.

The skilled bunter and speedy runner at first can put the run-and-bunt play on with amazing results. The bunter bunts the ball to third and makes baseman field the ball. The runner just keeps on going, and if the third is not alert, or the catcher is slow in covering third, he has an occasional to go to third base with one out. This was Pepper Martin's favourite play—but the bunter has to make the third baseman field the ball. A good time to execute this play is when the pitcher is behind in the count, and therefore more likely make the next pitch a strike. The best gained situation is with none, out a runner on first base.

Squeeze play

The safety and suicide squeeze plays are usually tried in the late innings with a runner on third base, one out, and the team at bat ahead, tied, or no more than one run behind.

Suicide squeeze

One of the dangers of the suicide squeeze is that, if the runner leaves too soon or gives the play away in any way, the first thing the pitcher will do is knock the hitter down. The hitter, or course, does not have a chance to bunt the ball, and the runner will very likely be tagged out at the plate. Ins', ad, the runner should wait until the pitcher's front foot hits the dirt, or until his arm starts coming through. Then, he cannot change the direction of his pitch. Now, it is up to the hitter to bunt the ball on the ground. It does not have to be a good bunt, merely on the ground, not too hard, but toward the pitcher. Many bunters, in this situation, try to lay down a perfect bunt. But the ball rolls foul and it defeats their purpose. If the runner starts at the Proper time, all that is necessary is for the ball to be bunted on the ground in fair territory.

To make sure nobody fouls up on his play, a "hold" sign is often given to the hitter, to be sure he gets it. He might answer by picking tip dirt and toss in it, pulling his belt, or using any simple signal!

Safety squeeze

The runner at third base should make his move only if the ball is bunted the ground. If the ball is popped up or missed, the runner does not go. A speedy runner should be on third when the safety squeeze is employed, because the runner must not start too soon. He waits to see where the ball is bunted, and then takes off. The ball is not bunted unless the pitch is a good one. The runner will try to score only if he thinks he can make it. A quick start is essential for the runner on third base.

Bunting

The bunting game is still an important part of a team's offensive strategy. Normally, the bunt is not used in the early innings of a game in these innings, most teams play for a big inning and do not sacrifice an out course, a bunt has more chance of working when the play is unexpected. In addition to being an effective weapon to move runners around, the bunt can be a surprise tactic to cross up defense. Players today are getting better each day at faking the bunt and then swinging the bat. This tends to keep the third baseman and the first baseman back just a little, and it helps. The ideal time for a squeeze play is with one out. If a manager has a good base runner on third and a pitcher is at the plate, he might to squeeze him in. If he lets the pitcher hit, he will more than likely strike or hit a double play. So, he has the pitcher lay one down.

Or, if the winning or tying run is on first base, the coach might want to get his runner down to second base and, in addition, score the man from third. So, he tries to bunt him over. He will tell his pitcher to bunt the ball down the third base line, with the idea of getting this runner to second case. As the third baseman comes in to field the ball, the runner at third should follow him in just a step or two behind him. If he throws to first base, a fast might have a good chance to score. Actually, this is not a squeeze play. Thee offense is just trying to get the man to second and not hit into a double pie.

Sacrifice bunt

The key rule in executing the sacrifice bunt is for the hitter to *give himself up.* On the straight sacrifice bunt, the batter attempts to bunt the ball only if the pitch is a strike. Late in a ball game, with the score tied or the team ore run behind, the manager probably wants to move over his runner on first base. He tells his hitter to bunt the ball down the first base line, because the first baseman has to hold the man on. Beside, the third baseman very likely would be right on top of the bunter.

To have the best chance at all to get the man over, the ',,inter has to bunt the ball down the first base line.

Of course, first basemen today often cheat a little and start running in before, the pitcher the ball, so unless the base runner can take an extra Step or two to (this, he could be in trouble. Since the sacrifice style of bunting would alert, the infielders, a hitter should not square around toward the pitcher until the very last instant. The drag bunt and push bunt are both attempts at a base hit. In bunting for a base hit, the hitter must know where the first baseman and third baseman are playing—if they are playing deep or shallow, and whether they are expecting the play. Some pitchers fall off the mound, so, if a right-hander falls off toward first, the bunt should be directed toward third base. If a left-hander keeps falling off to the left, the drag bunt could be aimed at the first baseman, in hopes that the bunter can beat the pitcher to first base.

A "hard bunt" or "slap bunt," is when the hitter squares around to bunt' but, instead, just slaps the ball. This is a pretty good challenge against the charging bunt defenses being used now.

Base running

Base running is controlled by the game situation. The number of outs, the score, the ability 'of the base runner, and the fielder's arm are factors that determine whether or not the runner attempts to advance. The batter and base runner must be alert to react quickly to passed balls, overthrows, and errors. Some pitchers have a good move to first base but a slow delivery. In this case, the runner cannot take as big a lead but he can still steal because he steals on the delivery. Other pitchers have a quicker delivery but a poor move to first base. Here, the runner should try to take a bigger lead because, when he throws to the plate, there won't be as much time. A pitcher who varies his tactics can be tough to steal on. He may quick-pitch occasionally Next, he will come to a set and then wait a long time before his pitch. On the next pitch, he will come in quickly.

Come to first

Base running begins at home plate. The ability to start quickly and get into running stride often spells the difference between a "safe" and an "out" call. No matter which side of the plate he swings from, the hitter should try to take his first step with the rear foot He must go hard for first, looking only at the bag, unless the coach signals or calls that the ball is through and for him to take his turn. There is nothing more disgusting than to see the batter hit the ball to the outfield or infield, and then watch the ball, and not put out full effort in going to first base. The infielder fumbles the ball, picks it up, and throws the hitter out by half step. Whereas, if lie had run Hie moment he hit the ball to first base, lie would have been safe by a full step. There is no excuse for a player not to run to first base. The only exception would be a pitcher at bat, on a hot day, in the seventh or eighth inning, after a tough inning of pitching.

The steal

If a team can use the steal successfully, they can eliminate the sacrifice. By stealing the base, the coach is much better off because, now, he does not have to sacrifice to *get* him there. The, steal is not only a great asset to the Defensive club, but it also rattles the pitcher and the fielders. The pitcher is so worried about the runner that he gets behind the hitter or makes a bad pitch. The second baseman or shortstop often has to "cheat" a little toward second base, so as to be there for the throw. Consequently, there is a wider gap to hit through.

The good base runner has to be aware of the pitchout. Usually, if a pitchout is executed properly, even runners as fast as Maury Wills and Willie Davis have trouble stealing the base, unless the pitcher's delivery is particularly slow. The count has to be right. Quite often, Maury would guess for a curve ball because it is better to steal on an off-speed pitch than on a fast ball.

The "steal" sign might be given the runner when fie is on second, or even third, but the runner goes only if fie gets a good jump. A good jump is the key to successful base running. A jump is leaving for the next base the instant the pitcher commits himself to delivering the ball to the plate. It is worth as much as two-tenths of a second. Instead of taking a seventeen-foot lead and attracting numerous throws, a top base-stealer may feel more comfortable with a fourteen or fifteen-foot lead, enabling him to get a better jump.

Double steal There are various types of double steals with runners on first and third. Some coaches start with the straight single steal from first base, while others use the break I before the pitch, delayed, or long-lead types. Here again, it depends on the pitcher.

If successful, this play can result in one run scored and a runner on second base. For example, the runner on first breaks for second on the pitch, and if the throw goes through to the base, he pulls up 'Short and becomes involved in a run-down situation. The man on third, meanwhile, waits until the thrown ball is over the pitcher's head before making his break for the plate.

Actually, the Dodgers do not use this type of double steal, in which we send a man from first and try to score the runner from third base. It often works at the high school level, but the major league defenses are too good for that. What happens, is that the catcher "looks" the runner back to third and then throws on to second base. If the runner starts too soon at third, he will be caught in a run-down play.

Sometimes, the defense might try to trick the runners by throwing directly back to the pitcher, and the offense would likely be in trouble. However, it is a gamble play, so the runner at third base will say to himself: "I will get as good a lead as I can. I will stand still, and wait until I see that the catcher has actually thrown the ball to second base."

Delayed steal The player with good speed who selects an opportunity to run should have a good chance of pulling off a delayed steal. The base runner should exploit any carelessness by the keystone combination, the pitcher or the catcher. The delayed steal is often tried with two outs, when the catcher has been lobbing the ball back to the pitcher, and the second baseman and shortstop are playing deep. Or, it is sometimes tried when the second baseman has a habit of looking down after the pitch is past the hitter.

The runner should break for second base the moment the catcher starts his throw to the Hitcher. The pitcher has to catch the ball, pivot, and throw, while the infielder who covers must come in from his deep position to make the play. One type of delayed might be used against a rookie Pitcher, especially a left-hander. As he comes down and gets set, the man on first base should start to run.

Although the pitcher knows there *is* a man on third base, if he is not concentrating at that particular moment, his first impulse is to back off, and he will likely throw to second base. The runner on third base knows this play is on, too, so he is creeping off; then, as soon as the pitcher backs off, he starts to go. Many times, if the pitcher makes only a motion toward second, the runner on third has a good chance to score before the pitcher can recover and throw to home.

The delayed steal should work particularly well at the college and high school levels. I do not think it should be used against a veteran pitcher, though, because he will step off the rubber and look to third before he commits himself to second base.

The natural impulse of many pitchers is to follow the runner. "There goes that runner!" Because he wants to do something about it, he steps off the slab and starts his motion to second or throws to get the runner in a run-down. Before the defense knows it, it is too late to stop the runner going home. If the pitcher does not step off, he will very likely balk. In fact, we have worked the delayed double steal a half dozen times in the major leagues, and it has proven to be a daring, tricky play that works. We have been caught only two or three times. However, a manager has to know how to pick his spots and situations.

Signals

The secret language of baseball is signals, and no team

gets very far without them. If a team is to win, a simple but effective system of communications must be set up. Flashing his signals from the bench or from the coaching lines, the manager or head coach can coordinate individual efforts into team action. Signs, in the case of young players, can be quite simple and few in number, while signs with older and more experienced players can cover more situations and plays. Whatever the system, each member of the squad should know the signs perfectly. Too many signs on a team can be worse than none at all. A baseball player may have enough trouble keeping his mind on the game situation, without having to worry about a long, complicated series of signals. As Yogi Berra once said, "How can you hit and *think* at the same time?" Yogi, of course, was exaggerating the situation, but it is true that a player must concentrate on the task at hand, whether it be hitting or fielding. Signals that take too much mental effort to comprehend should not be used. They should be simple. Unquestionably, the effectiveness of signals depends upon their execution. A simple set of signs, combined with an indicator or key, plus some motions for camouflage can be most difficult for tile opposition to intercept. Any natural movement of the cap, hands, or arms, mixed in with other natural actions, will do the trick

Actually, the causes of missed signals are quite simple. The player did not look at the coach, he did not look at the right time or the manager did not give the signal properly There is no excuse for a player not to know the signs, even if they are somewhat complicated. He has all his free time to learn the signals.

After the signals are used awhile, there should be no missed signs. That is the trouble with the "flash" sign. If the manager gives a "flash" sign and the player does not happen to be looking at the right time, he does have an excuse. However, the first time the hitter turns around and looks at the coach, the coach should give a "yes" or "no." "Yes—I'm going to give you a sign," or, "No—I won't." For instance, if the coach rubs down below the belt, it means, "No, there is not a sign." If he rubs anything above the belt, the player has to be alert, because a sign will be given. As soon as the coach hits the key with one hand, he will give the sign with the other hand.

A simpler set of signs should be given a high school player—more holding signs, such as hands on the knees belt, keeping them there a little longer. The coach should either face him, walk toward him, or walk away from him. It is more important to, have the players sure that they get the sign, rather than be too concerned about the opposing club stealing them.

Coaches should be pretty good actors. They have to make some kind of movement or signal-giving motion on practically every pitch. They should do a lot of faking constantly, so that, when they do give a sign, it is not obvious.

Practice

The manager or coach should not be satisfied just to go over the signs with his team and let it go at that, Sufficient practice time should be devoted to executing them until they are well understood. They should be used in all intrasquad games, with the coaches performing their duties on the base lines under typical game conditions.

INDEX